Diet recommendations for rheumatic joint diseases

Please check these recommendations always with a nutrition consultant, therapist, doctor or dietician. The recipes and the list of ingredients are supporting the conventional medical therapy.
The calorie disclosures of fresh ingredients (fruit and vegetables) vary according to quality and time of harvest. The contents were checked by a dietician and a nutrition consultant for the Traditional Chinese Medicine (TCM).

Author:
©2019 Josef Miligui
www.ebns.at

AF198748

Source:
The lists are created from the EBNS database for nutritional counseling. The database is used by dietitians, therapists and doctors for advising the patient / client.

Literature:
The specialist literature and the training documents of the German and Austrian dietary and traditional Chinese medicine serve as a knowledge base. We have used the documents as a basis of knowledge, adapted it to our experience and completed them.
http://di-book.com

Production and publishing:
BoD – Books on Demand, Norderstedt
ISBN: 9783746043296

Diet recommendations for DIETETICS - special diseases - Rheumatic joint diseases

1 Treatment strategy

Five servings of fruits and vegetables per day as well as regular consumption of pods provide the body with sufficient antioxidants such as vitamin C, vitamin E, beta-carotene and selenium.
These substances absorb aggressive oxygen radicals, which are increasingly formed during inflammatory processes.
Use valuable vegetable oils such as rapeseed, soy and walnut oil and a vitamin E-rich spread fat such as margarine.
Two sea-fish meals per week can also have a positive effect on the disease due to the favorable fatty acid composition.
Salmon, herring and mackerel in particular contain large amounts of omega-3 fatty acids, which have an anti-inflammatory effect.

2 Avoid

Fat-rich animal products such as sausage, various types of meat, butter and cheese should be rarely and in small quantities on the menu.
They contain arachidonic acid from which inflammation-promoting messengers are formed.
Alcohol and nicotine.

3 Breakfast

kkal. per serving

Basic recipe for a vegetable soup, nutritious 47
Cranberry juice 43
Cucumber soup 95
Fried apple 408
Hungarian rice salad 421
Lettuce with vinegar dressing 67
Noodles with Vegetable and tomato sauce 561
Oat flakes with aromatic spices 280
Plum Cake 502

4   Snack

5   Lunch

6 Afternoon

7 Dinner

8   Any time

9 Recipes

(rec.) = You can use more.
(little) = You should use less than specified
(no) omit.

9.1 Andalusian fish pot

Strengthens immune system, prevents cancer, dissolves stagnation, promotes weight loss. Good to fight immunodeficiency, loss of appetite, flatulence, high blood pressure, depressions, diabetes, diarrhea, stimulates appetite.
Cooking time approx. 30 min
Allergens: ADLO
4 portions to 355g. / 348kcal. - (carb:71% / prot:29%)
100g.=97,96kcal. / protein 20,03g. fat:6,51g.
µg. - Ph:3,89 Na:5,05 Ka:8,67 Mg:3,36 Ca:10,73 Fe:0,03 Zn:0,02 Col.:0,79 Hsr.:2,47

Quantity of ingredients:
Basic recipe for a vegetable soup (nutritious) 2 cups / 500g. (yes)
Onion (spring onion) 2 pieces / 40g. (yes)
Olive oil 1 table spoon / 20g. (yes)
Lemon peel 1/2 piece / 3g. (yes)
Bay leaf 1 piece / 1g. (yes)
Potato 5/8 oz / 200g. (yes)
Cod 3/4 lbs / 300g. (rec.)
White wine 4 table spoons / 80g. (little)
Lemon juice 1/2 teaspoon / 10g. (yes)
Salt 1 pinch / 1g. (little)
Pepper (ground) 1 pinch / 0,2g. ()
Parsley 1 table spoon / 15g. (yes)
White bread (wheat bread) 8 slices / 250g. (yes)

Cooking instructions:
Boil the vegetable broth with small spring onion, olive oil, grated lemon peel and bay leaf. Boil covered for 10 minutes. Add the peeled, diced potatoes and boil in about 8 minutes. Add fish pieces and white wine and switch to small heat. In the slightly boiling broth put the fish and boil it a few minutes. Season with lemon juice, salt and pepper. Serve with parsley sprinkled.
White bread as a side dish.

9.2 Asparagus and herb ragout

Diuretic, improves blood circulation, prevents cancer, dissolves stagnation, promotes weight loss. Good to fight immunodeficiency, loss of appetite, flatulence, high blood pressure, depressions, diabetes, diarrhea, stimulates liver function.

Cooking time approx. 30 min

Allergens: GL

4 portions to 465,5g. / 168kcal. - (carb:78% / prot:22%)
100g.=36,14kcal. / protein 7,54g. fat:4,09g.
µg. - Ph:2,55 Na:0,54 Ka:11,94 Mg:2,69 Ca:9,45 Fe:0,06 Zn:0,02 Col.:0 Hsr.:1,09

Quantity of ingredients:
Basic recipe for a vegetable soup (nutritious) 2 cups / 500g. (yes)
Lemon peel 1/2 piece / 3g. (yes)
Coriander 1/4 teaspoon / 1g. (yes)
Nutmeg 1 pinch / 0,3g. (yes)
Asparagus (green or white) 1,8 lbs / 800g. (yes)
Parsley 1 Bunch / 125g. (yes)
Crème fraiche cheese 2 table spoons / 30g. (little)
Lemon juice 1 teaspoon / 3g. (yes)
Potato 7/8 lbs / 400g. (yes)

Cooking instructions:
Cook potatoes with plenty of salted water about 20 min. until soft.
Heat the vegetable stock with lemon zest, coriander and nutmeg till it boil. Cook the peeled and sliced asparagus in it.
Drain asparagus in a sieve. Collect the cooking liquid.
In the blender mix 200 g of cooked asparagus (the lower ends), cooking liquid and parsley to a smooth sauce. Beat the sauce with crème fraîche until smooth. Add asparagus and heat again and season with lemon juice, salt and pepper. Serve with the potatoes.

9.3 Asparagus Cream Soup

Diuretic, improves blood circulation, prevents cancer, laxative, antiparasitic, stimulates liver function, good to fight loss of appetite, flatulence, rheumatism, heartburn.

Cooking time approx. 45 min

Allergens: ACG

2 portions to 409,5g. / 240kcal. - (carb:21% / prot:79%)
100g.=58,61kcal. / protein 5,2g. fat:19,85g.
µg. - Ph:9,44 Na:1,5 Ka:15,8 Mg:1,6 Ca:6,23 Fe:0,13 Zn:0,08 Col.:9,84 Hsr.:2,42

Quantity of ingredients:
Asparagus (green or white) 5/8 oz / 200g. (yes)
Water 2 cup / 500g. (yes)
Rapeseed oil 3 table spoons / 30g. (rec.)
Wheat flour 2 table spoons / 10g. (yes)
Chicken yolk 1 piece / 25g. (little)
Cow's milk (whole milk 3.5% fat) 1 table spoon / 15g. (little)
Sour cream 15% fat 1 table spoon / 15g. (little)
Pepper (ground) 1 pinch / 0,5g. ()
Nutmeg 1 pinch / 0,5g. (yes)
Lemon juice 1 teaspoon / 2g. (yes)
Parsley 2 table spoons / 20g. (yes)
Salt 1 pinch / 1g. (little)

Cooking instructions:
Wash and peel the asparagus.
Heat water, a little lemon juice and pinch of salt till it boils. Tie the asparagus spears together.
Add the asparagus peel to the cooking water and bring to the boil.
Add the asparagus and cook on low heat for about 20 minutes.
Then remove the asparagus bunches and pour the broth through a sieve.
For the roux, heat the oil in a saucepan, add the flour and sauté until it is colorless, slowly top up with the asparagus sauce and simmer for 10 minutes. Cut the asparagus spears into pieces about 3 cm long and place them to the soup.

Just before serving, bring the soup to the boil again.
Mix the egg yolk with the milk and sour cream.
Remove the pot from the heat and stir in the egg yolk and milk mixture.
Season with pepper and nutmeg, decorate with the chopped parsley and serve immediately.

9.4   Basic recipe for a reissue soup (Congee)

Low fat content, for the drainage of the body overweight and high blood pressure.
Cooking time approx. 2-4 hours
3 portions to 273,33g. / 140kcal. - (carb:90% / prot:10%)
100g.=51,34kcal. / protein 2,96g. fat:0,48g.
µg. - Ph:1,95 Na:0,19 Ka:1,67 Mg:1,14 Ca:0,57 Fe:0,01 Zn:0,02 Col.:0 Hsr.:2,11

Quantity of ingredients:
Rice variety any 1 cup / 120g. (yes)
Water 6 cups / 700g. (yes)

Cooking instructions:
Cook rice and water in a ratio of about 1: 6. The amount of water determines the thickness of the mash (matter of taste).
Put the rice in a saucepan with a heavy lid. It is important to simmer the rice after a short boil on the slightest flame, otherwise it burns.
Boil the rice for 2-4 hours. The longer he cooks, the more he strengthens.
If you want to eat the dish for breakfast, you can put the rice on just before bedtime.
To be on the safe side, you should first check the behavior of your pot and cooker under observation for a similar amount of time, so that nothing burns.
Refrigerate for later use.

9.5   Basic recipe for a vegetable soup, nutritious

Reduces blood pressure, strengthens immune system, prevents cancer, forcing spleen, dissolves stagnation, promotes weight loss. Good to fight immunodeficiency, high blood pressure, depressions, diabetes, diarrhea, reduces blood lipids.
Cooking time approx. 2-3 hours
Allergens: L
5 portions to 240,6g. / 48kcal. - (carb:71% / prot:29%)
100g.=19,87kcal. / protein 1,56g. fat:1,31g.
µg. - Ph:0,97 Na:0,73 Ka:5,14 Mg:0,36 Ca:1,26 Fe:0,02 Zn:0,01 Col.:0 Hsr.:0,56

Quantity of ingredients:
Olive oil 1 table spoon / 4g. (yes)
Onion white 1 piece / 60g. (yes)
Carrot 3 pieces / 200g. (yes)
Parsnip 3/8 lbs - 6oz / 150g. (yes)
Celery root 1 cup / 100g. (yes)
Ginger fresh 1/2 teaspoon / 2g. (yes)
Lemon 1/2 piece / 25g. (yes)
Juniper berry 6 pieces / 6g. (yes)
Thyme dried 1 pinch / 1g. (yes)
Lovage 1 table spoon / 3g. (yes)
Bay leaf 2 leaves / 1g. (yes)
Salt 1 pinch / 1g. (little)
Water 3 cups / 650g. (yes)

Cooking instructions:
Cut the vegetables into cubes.
Heat oil in hot pot, fry shortly onions and vegetables.
Add cold water, then add ginger, bay leaf and lemon juice.
Season with juniper, thyme and lovage. Cover for 2 - 3 hours on a low heat and simmer.
The used vegetables should be thrown away.
The basic recipe serves as a soup base and to refine vegetables, legumes or cereals.
If you want to eat vegetable soup immediately, add the desired vegetables half an hour before.
Refrigerate for later use.

9.6   Beef pumpkin and vegetable stew

Reduces inflammation, improves digestion, reduces blood glucose, strengthens the muscles, tendons and bones, promotes digestion, helps to digest fat.
Cooking time approx. 1 hour
Allergens: AL
4 portions to 403,75g. / 369kcal. - (carb:48% / prot:52%)
100g.=91,46kcal. / protein 30,38g. fat:11,37g.
µg. - Ph:4,56 Na:3,23 Ka:16,05 Mg:1,7 Ca:3,71 Fe:0,08 Zn:0,08 Col.:1 Hsr.:2,83

Quantity of ingredients:
Beef meat 3/4 lbs / 350g. (little)
Pumpkin 3/4 lbs / 350g. (yes)
Leek 3/8 lbs - 6oz / 150g. (yes)
Potato 3/4 lbs / 350g. (yes)
Tomato 3/8 lbs - 6oz / 150g. (yes)
Olive oil 2 table spoons / 25g. (yes)
Basic recipe for a vegetable soup (nutritious) 1/4 lbs - 4oz / 125g. (yes)
Salt 1 pinch / 1g. (little)
Pepper (ground) 1 pinch / 0,5g. ()
Peppers powder 1 teaspoon / 2g. (yes)
Ground caraway 1 pinch / 1g. (yes)
Sugar cane sugar 1 pinch / 1g. (little)
Parsley 1/2 bunch / 30g. (yes)
White bread (wheat bread) 4 slices / 80g. (yes)

Cooking instructions:
Dice beef. Peel pumpkin and dice. Cut the leek into rings and dice the peeled potatoes.
Brew the tomatoes with boiling water, peel off the skin and dice.
Steam the meat in olive oil and fill with vegetable stock. Add the cleaned vegetables. Season with salt, pepper, paprika, cumin and fructose.
Stew for 30 minutes over low heat.
Season again and sprinkle with parsley and serve with white bread.

9.7 Cranberry juice

Antibacterial, good to fight loss of appetite, arteriosclerosis, bladder infections, diarrhea, colds. Antipyretic, against free radicals, gout, diuretic, stomach ulcers, oral mucosa inflammation, rheumatism.
Cooking time approx. 5 min
1 portion to 160g. / 43kcal. - (carb:98% / prot:2%)
100g.=26,88kcal. / protein 0,14g. fat:0,02g.
µg. - Ph:2,06 Na:1,53 Ka:11,69 Mg:1,16 Ca:4,22 Fe:0,09 Zn:0,09 Col.:0 Hsr.:3,12

Quantity of ingredients:
Cranberries 2 table spoons / 25g. (yes)
Water 1 cup / 125g. (yes)
Honey 1 table spoon / 10g. (yes)

Cooking instructions:
Mix the cranberries with a little water with the blender to a pulp. Add the remaining water and sweeten with the honey.

9.8 Cucumber soup

Diuretic, detoxifying, suppresses conversion of sugar into fat, lowers cholesterol, prevents cancer, promotes digestion, diaphoretic, dries out, good to fight yeast infections.
Cooking time approx. 20 min
Allergens: M
4 portions to 235,25g. / 96kcal. - (carb:22% / prot:78%)
100g.=40,6kcal. / protein 0,91g. fat:9,03g.
µg. - Ph:2,67 Na:1,28 Ka:15,6 Mg:1,17 Ca:2,57 Fe:0,06 Zn:0,01 Col.:0 Hsr.:0,85

Quantity of ingredients:
Olive oil 2 table spoons / 35g. (yes)
Cucumber 2 pieces / 400g. (yes)
Water 2 cup / 500g. (yes)
Sage 3 leaves / 3g. (yes)
Mustard 1/2 teaspoon / 0,5g. (rec.)
Coriander 1 pinch / 1g. (yes)
Cardamom 1 pinch / 1g. (yes)
Salt 1 pinch / 1g. (little)

Cooking instructions:
Heat oil and roast short the small cucumbers. Add Mustard seeds, coriander, cardamom and salt. Add water. Simmer for 10-15 min. Puree and decorate with fresh chopped sage.

9.9 Fried apple

Good to fight acute or chronic constipation of the intestine, warming stomach and spleen, improves blood circulation. Good to fight kidney weakness, back pain and abdominal pain, impotence.
Cooking time approx. 30 min
Allergens: GH
4 portions to 353,5g. / 408kcal. - (carb:51% / prot:49%)
100g.=115,42kcal. / protein 11,89g. fat:22,21g.
µg. - Ph:5,08 Na:1,79 Ka:11,92 Mg:1,37 Ca:5,71 Fe:0,03 Zn:0,03 Col.:4,65 Hsr.:0,51

Quantity of ingredients:
Apple (sour) 4 pieces / 500g. (yes)
Hazelnuts 1/8 lbs - 2oz / 50g. (yes)
Almond 1/8 lbs - 2oz / 50g. (yes)
Cinnamon ground 1 pinch / 0,2g. (yes)
Vanilla sugar natural 1 package / 3g. (yes)
Cow's milk (whole milk 3.5% fat) 2 table spoons / 24g. (little)
Sugar - icing sugar 3 table spoons / 36g. (little)
Cinnamon ground 1 pinch / 1g. (yes)
Yoghurt vanilla 3 cups / 750g. (little)

Cooking instructions:
Wash the apples, cut off a lid, cut out the core casing with a teaspoon so that the apple remains a tight bottom.
Mix nuts, almonds, fructose, milk, vanilla sugar, cinnamon well. Fill into

the apples. Put the covers back on.
Bake in preheated oven at 180 ° C for approx. 20 minutes.
Mix icing sugar and cinnamon.
Spread vanilla yoghurt on plate, place 1 baked apple on each, sprinkle with cinnamon-powdered sugar mixture. Serve hot immediately!

9.10 Grilled salmon steaks with cauliflower and potatoes

Improves digestion, regenerates skin, supports urination, lowers cholesterol, supports digestion.
Cooking time approx. 30 min
Allergens: D
4 portions to 436,75g. / 330kcal. - (carb:33% / prot:67%)
100g.=75,5kcal. / protein 33,21g. fat:24,12g.
µg. - Ph:26,67 Na:5,17 Ka:77 Mg:4,82 Ca:3,58 Fe:0,16 Zn:0,1 Col.:2,51 Hsr.:16,78

Quantity of ingredients:
Garlic 1 clove / 1g. (yes)
Onion (shallot) 1/2 piece / 5g. (yes)
Lemon juice 1 splash / 1g. (yes)
Salt 1 pinch / 1g. (little)
Cauliflower 1 piece / 500g. (yes)
Olive oil 2 table spoons / 20g. (yes)
Garlic 1 clove / 1g. (yes)
Water 2/3 cup / 200g. (yes)
Parsley 3 table spoons / 15g. (yes)
Potato 1,1 lbs / 500g. (yes)
Salt 1 pinch / 1g. (little)
Salmon 4 pieces (steaks) / 500g. (rec.)
Lemon 1/2 piece / 2g. (yes)

Cooking instructions:
Garlic shallots mixture:
Finely squeeze the garlic, finely chop the shallots, add a dash of lemon juice and salt and stir. Mix with a little oil to a paste.
Cauliflower:
Cut the cauliflower into pieces.
Heat the oil in a heavy saucepan and fry the crushed garlic for a short time.
Add the cauliflower pieces and turn in the oil. Add a little water and cook until the cauliflower is firm. Strain the cauliflower and cook the remaining water until a thick sauce remains. Add the cauliflower and crush it roughly with a wooden spoon. Add the chopped parsley and

salt.

Potatoes:

Cook the potato in a saucepan with plenty of water, strain and peel.

Salmon Steak:

Preheat the oven at about 180°C/356°F. Rub in the salmon slices with the garlic-scarlet mixture and grill as close as possible to the heat source for 4 to 8 minutes from both sides. You are done when the meat is easy to divide when you pierce with a fork.

Serve and sprinkle with lemon slices and the chopped parsley.

9.11 Grilled tomatoes with cheese filling

Promotes digestion, helps to digest fat, supports urination, reduces blood pressure, stimulates digestion.

Cooking time approx. 30 min

Allergens: ACG

2 portions to 319,5g. / 470kcal. - (carb:38% / prot:62%)
100g.=146,95kcal. / protein 18,89g. fat:30,98g.
µg. - Ph:25,05 Na:101,57 Ka:41,33 Mg:3,14 Ca:21,11 Fe:0,17 Zn:0,12 Col.:13,64
Hsr.:4,36

Quantity of ingredients:
Tomato 8 pieces / 200g. (yes)
Feta cheese 0,2 lbs / 75g. (little)
Fresh cheese 0,2 lbs / 75g. (little)
Chicken egg 1 piece / 60g. (little)
Olive oil 1 table spoon / 12g. (yes)
Basil (fresh) 1 table spoon / 6g. (yes)
Salt 1 pinch / 1g. (little)
Pepper (ground) 1 pinch / 0,5g. ()
Olives 1 oz / 30g. (yes)
Rucola 1/4 lbs / 100g. ()
White bread (wheat bread) 4 slices / 80g. (yes)

Cooking instructions:
Hollow out tomatoes generously. Put in a casserole dish.

Mix cheese, olive oil, egg, chopped basil and flour. Season with salt and pepper and fill in the tomatoes.

Bake in the preheated oven at 210 degrees on the middle rail for 15 minutes, then switch on the oven grill and grill for a further 3 minutes (without circulating air).

Stone the olives and chop and sprinkle on the tomatoes.

Garnish tomatoes with rocket and serve with white bread.

9.12 Halibut with tomato and garlic sauce

Promotes digestion, helps to digest fat, supports urination, reduces blood pressure, good to fight rheumatism, flatulence, bladder weakness, anemia, high blood pressure, depressions, diabetes, diarrhea. Valuable omega-3 fatty acids.

Cooking time approx. 45 min

Allergens: D

5 portions to 297,6g. / 319kcal. - (carb:36% / prot:64%)
100g.=107,19kcal. / protein 34,96g. fat:9,44g.
µg. - Ph:4,82 Na:8,78 Ka:7,08 Mg:1,03 Ca:0,88 Fe:0,02 Zn:0,01 Col.:0,82 Hsr.:4,78

Quantity of ingredients:
Rice variety any 1 cup / 120g. (yes)
Water 6 cups / 240g. (yes)
Salt 1 pinch / 1g. (little)
Halibut (Flatfish) 2,2 lbs / 800g. (rec.)
Salt 1 pinch / 1g. (little)
Pepper (ground) 1 pinch / 0,5g. ()
Lemon juice 1 splash / 2g. (yes)
Bay leaf 2 pieces / 2g. (yes)
Lemon 1 piece / 30g. (yes)
Garlic 8 pieces / 10g. (yes)
Thyme dried 1 table spoon / 5g. (yes)
Olives 0,2 lbs / 75g. (yes)
Tomato 4 pieces / 200g. (yes)
Salt 1 pinch / 1g. (little)
Pepper (ground) 1 pinch / 0,5g. ()

Cooking instructions:
Cook rice with salted water (1:3).
Rinse the fish under running cold water, dab with kitchen paper and rub with salt, pepper and lemon juice.
Place the fish fillets in a casserole dish with pieces of bay leaf.

Wash the lemon hot and cut into slices, peel and halve the garlic.
Sprinkle the olives and the thyme over them.
Brew the tomatoes with hot water, skin and chop.

Mix all ingredients, season with salt and pepper and distribute around the fish.

Cook everything at 200°C/392°F for about 20 minutes.
Serve with the rice.

9.13 Hungarian rice salad

Promotes digestion, helps to digest fat, supports urination, reduces blood pressure, strengthens kidney and bladder, diuretic, warming the body from the inside, expands blood vessels, strengthens the muscles, regulates internal organs functions.
Cooking time approx. 25 min
Allergens: GM
2 portions to 323,5g. / 421kcal. - (carb:54% / prot:46%)
100g.=130,14kcal. / protein 8,23g. fat:14,84g.
µg. - Ph:18,97 Na:10,25 Ka:26,18 Mg:5,55 Ca:14,42 Fe:0,12 Zn:0,11 Col.:0,77 Hsr.:4,63

Quantity of ingredients:
Rice (whole grain) 1/2 cup / 60g. (yes)
Water 3 cups / 300g. (yes)
Salt 1 pinch / 0,3g. (little)
Tomato 1/4 lbs - 4oz / 100g. (yes)
Peppers 1/8 lbs - 2oz / 50g. (rec.)
Champignon 1 oz / 30g. (yes)
Edam cheese 1 oz / 30g. (little)
Yogurt (natural, 1.5% fat) 1/8 lbs - 2oz / 45g. (yes)
Salt 1 pinch / 1g. (little)
Herbs various 1 table spoon / 8g. (yes)
Rapeseed oil 2 table spoons / 20g. (rec.)
Mustard 1 teaspoon / 3g. (rec.)
Pepper (ground) 1 pinch / 0,2g. ()

Cooking instructions:
Pour the rice into plenty of boiling salt water and let it drain gently. Wash tomatoes and peppers and core. Cut both in to small cubes. Peel the mushrooms (from the tin or with rapeseed oil for a short time) and cut the cheese into small cubes and add to the rice. Prepare the marinade and mix with the ingredients, refrigerate and leave for at least an hour.

9.14 Lasagne with tofu cream

Harmonizes spleen and stomach, reduces Flatulence, protects the digestive system. Good to fight lack of appetite, flatulence, inflammatory bowel disease, stomach ulcers, rheumatism, heartburn, twelffinger intestinal ulcers.

Cooking time approx. 45 min
Allergens: ACEG
4 portions to 231g. / 301kcal. - (carb:50% / prot:50%)
100g.=130,3kcal. / protein 19,33g. fat:11,88g.
µg. - Ph:8,79 Na:3,51 Ka:7,05 Mg:4,06 Ca:7,27 Fe:0,09 Zn:0,05 Col.:3,83 Hsr.:3,82

Quantity of ingredients:
Soy Tofu 7/8 lbs / 400g. (yes)
Chicken egg 2 pieces / 100g. (little)
Onion white 2 pieces / 120g. (yes)
Tomato 1/4 lbs - 4oz / 100g. (yes)
Oregano dried 1 pinch / 1g. (yes)
Marjoram 1 pinch / 1g. (yes)
Peppers powder 1 pinch / 1g. (yes)
Salt 1 pinch / 1g. (little)
Noodles (wheat, lasagne) with egg 3/8 lbs - 6oz / 150g. (little)
Edam cheese 1/8 lbs - 2oz / 50g. (little)

Cooking instructions:
Tofu cream: Mix tofu with eggs, onions, small tomatoes, oregano, marjoram, peppers and some sea salt put into a smooth mass using a kitchen machine with a knife or a blender.

Lasagne: Place 1/5 of the tofu cream in a casserole dish (25x15cm), cover with 3 lasagna leaves, repeat this process twice, and then finish the last fifth of the tofu cream over the pastry plates. Sprinkle with a little grated Edam and bake in the oven at 175°C/347°F for about 1/2 hour.

9.15 Lettuce with fresh cheese

The bitter substances have diuretic effect and promote the blood circulation in the digestive area. Mustard improves thyroid function, relieves rheumatism symptoms.
Cooking time approx. 5 min
Allergens: AFM
1 portion to 260g. / 802kcal. - (carb:21% / prot:79%)
100g.=308,46kcal. / protein 22,11g. fat:52,97g.
µg. - Ph:138,82 Na:313,1 Ka:257,72 Mg:28,88 Ca:84,62 Fe:0,54 Zn:0,48 Col.:0,06
Hsr.:14,65

Quantity of ingredients:
Leaf salads (bitter) 2 portions / 60g. (yes)
Fresh cheese from soya 3/8 lbs - 6oz / 150g. (rec.)
Mustard 1 knife tip / 1g. (rec.)
Lemon juice 1 dash / 3g. (yes)

Salt 1 pinch / 1g. (little)
Pepper (ground) 1 pinch / 0,5g. ()
Herbs various 2 teaspoons / 4g. (yes)
Black caraway 1 pinch / 1g. (yes)
Whole grain bread 2 slices / 40g. (yes)

Cooking instructions:
Wash lettuce and finely pluck.
Mix 150 ml cream cheese, splashes of mustard, splashes of lemon juice, 1 clove of garlic, chopped fresh herbs, pinch of pepper and crushed black cumin and pour over. Serve with wholemeal bread.

9.16 Lettuce with vinegar dressing

Relieves fatigue, regulates gastrointestinal function, dissolves stagnation, laxative, antiparasitic, improves blood circulation, detoxifying, reduces inflammation, relieves pain.
Cooking time approx. 10 min
Allergens: O
2 portions to 127,5g. / 68kcal. - (carb:32% / prot:68%)
100g.=52,94kcal. / protein 1,64g. fat:4,88g.
µg. - Ph:8,07 Na:2,56 Ka:49,71 Mg:2,9 Ca:8,86 Fe:0,22 Zn:0,09 Col.:0 Hsr.:5

Quantity of ingredients:
Lettuce 1 piece / 200g. (yes)
Vinegar (Apple vinegar) 1 table spoon / 10g. (yes)
Water 1 table spoon / 10g. (yes)
Rapeseed oil 1 table spoon / 10g. (rec.)
Onion (spring onion) 1 piece / 20g. (yes)
Salt 1 pinch / 0,5g. (little)
Pepper (ground) 1 pinch / 0,1g. ()
Chives 1 table spoon / 5g. (yes)

Cooking instructions:
Clean lettuce, wash and drain. Add the ingredients to the marinade in an extra container. Salad with marinade just before consumption. Just before, sprinkle with chives.

9.17 Marinated cod on pumpkin puree

Reduces inflammation, improves digestion, promotes spleen, lung, stomach and kidneys, diuretic, reduces blood glucose, good to fight constipation and flatulence, dissolves stagnation.
Cooking time approx. 2 hours
Allergens: DG
4 portions to 288,5g. / 202kcal. - (carb:49% / prot:51%)
100g.=69,84kcal. / protein 17,24g. fat:5,13g.
µg. - Ph:5,4 Na:2,01 Ka:17,22 Mg:1,4 Ca:2,11 Fe:0,03 Zn:0,02 Col.:1,02 Hsr.:2,55

Quantity of ingredients:
Potato 6 pieces / 400g. (yes)
Pumpkin 5/8 oz / 200g. (yes)
Onion white 1 piece / 50g. (yes)
Oregano dried 1/2 teaspoon / 1g. (yes)
Lemon juice 1/2 piece / 15g. (yes)
Salt 1 pinch / 1g. (little)
Pepper (ground) 1 pinch / 0,3g. ()
Crème fraiche cheese 2 table spoons / 30g. (little)
Yogurt (natural, 1.5% fat) 3/8 lbs - 6oz / 150g. (yes)
Oregano dried 1/4 teaspoon / 1g. (yes)
Basil (fresh) 1/2 teaspoon / 2g. (yes)
Cod 3/4 lbs / 300g. (rec.)
Salt 1 pinch / 1g. (little)
Pepper (ground) 1 pinch / 0,3g. ()
Olive oil 1 teaspoon / 3g. (yes)

Cooking instructions:
Mix yoghurt with oregano, basil and thyme. Wash the fish fillets, pat dry, place in a flat shape and pour over the marinade. Leave 2 hours in refrigerator.

Cook the potatoes in salted water until soft and peel.

Sauté the onion in oil until glassy, add the diced pumpkin and cook for about 10 min. Add oregano, lemon juice, salt, pepper and creme fraiche and puree with the blender.

Remove fish fillets from the marinade, drain, pat dry and salt. Coat a coated grill pan with 2 teaspoons of oil. Roast the fish fillets on both sides for 3 - 4 minutes and arrange with the potatoes on the pumpkin puree.

9.18 Noodles with turkeymeat and pineapple

Solves bile-, kidney- and bladder stones, provides Vitamin C, strengthens blood, strengthens bone marrow, reduces inflammation, supports urination.
Cooking time approx. 45 min
Allergens: ACGL
4 portions to 333g. / 292kcal. - (carb:53% / prot:47%)
100g.=87,61kcal. / protein 17,59g. fat:11,45g.
µg. - Ph:5,54 Na:3,01 Ka:12,71 Mg:1,78 Ca:4,2 Fe:0,05 Zn:0,05 Col.:0,98 Hsr.:3,07

Quantity of ingredients:
Noodles (whole grain) with egg 5/8 oz / 200g. (little)
Pineapple 5/8 oz / 200g. (yes)
Water 1/2 cup / 50g. (yes)
Turkey breast meat 5/8 oz / 200g. (yes)
Rapeseed oil 1 table spoon / 12g. (rec.)
Garlic 1 piece / 2g. (yes)
Basic recipe for a vegetable soup (nutritious) 1/2 cup / 100g. (yes)
Cow's milk (whole milk 3.5% fat) 2/3 cup / 180g. (little)
Fresh cheese 0,2 lbs / 75g. (little)
Curry 3 teaspoons / 6g. (yes)
Salt 1 pinch / 1g. (little)
Pepper (ground) 1 pinch / 0,5g. ()
Pomegranate 1 piece / 300g. (yes)
Coconut flakes 1 table spoon / 6g. (yes)

Cooking instructions:
Cook the noodles in salt water. Cut the pineapple into cubes and leave for 5 min. to simmer in water. Cut the meat sliced in strips and roast them in the oil. Add the chopped garlic and the pineapple sliced. Add about 50 ml of the pineapple juice and stir in the vegetable broth. Add the milk and the fresh cheese, then stir well until the fresh cheese is completely dissolved. Now add the curry and simmer for a few minutes until a creamy consistency is reached. Season with salt and pepper. Now add the noodles in the finished sauce. Cut the pomegranate and release the seeds. Distribute as many kernels on the dressed noodles. Whoever likes it can spread coconut chips over it.

9.19 Noodles with vegetable and tomato sauce

Protects the digestive system. Detoxifying, Good to fight loss of appetite, flatulence, inflammatory bowel disease, obesity, gout, stomach ulcers, stomach cramps, rheumatism, heartburn, twelffinger intestinal ulcers, promotes digestion, helps to digest fat.

Cooking time approx. 45 min

Allergens: ACG

2 portions to 281g. / 562kcal. - (carb:70% / prot:30%)
100g.=199,82kcal. / protein 14,06g. fat:21,68g.
µg. - Ph:21,13 Na:3,21 Ka:44,61 Mg:8,06 Ca:6,77 Fe:0,3 Zn:0,2 Col.:8,37 Hsr.:18,02

Quantity of ingredients:
Tomato 1/4 lbs - 4oz / 125g. (yes)
Carrot 1 piece / 80g. (yes)
Zucchini 1 piece / 80g. (yes)
Olive oil 1 table spoon / 15g. (yes)
Onion (shallot) 1 piece / 20g. (yes)
Oregano dried 1 pinch / 1g. (yes)
Salt 1 pinch / 1g. (little)
Pepper (ground) 1 pinch / 0,2g. ()
Noodles (wheat) with egg 5/8 oz / 200g. (little)
Olive oil 1 table spoon / 10g. (yes)
Crème fraiche cheese 2 table spoons / 30g. (little)

Cooking instructions:
Boil the tomatoes with a little water, drain and collect the juice, cut the tomatoes into pieces.
Roughly grate zucchini and carrot. Heat olive oil in a pot. Steam shallots very soft. Add tomatoes, season with oregano, salt and pepper. Simmer tomatoes to a thick sauce.
Bring plenty of salted water to boil, cook the wholegrain noodles until firm. In the cooking time of the pasta, heat in a pan olive oil. Fry the carrots while stirring, lightly salt. Add zucchini, sauté
briefly while stirring. The vegetables should be soft with a bite.
Drain pasta, mix with crème fraiche, season with salt and pepper.
Garnish with the tomato sauce.

9.20 Oat flakes with aromatic spices

Stops diarrhea, promotes digestion, appetizing, harmonizes the stomach, relieves diarrhea, strengthens immune system, detoxifying and stimulating the immune system.
Cooking time approx. 25 min
Allergens: AH
3 portions to 208g. / 280kcal. - (carb:69% / prot:31%)
100g.=134,78kcal. / protein 6,73g. fat:10,72g.
µg. - Ph:11,3 Na:0,78 Ka:17,25 Mg:4,26 Ca:2,68 Fe:0,15 Zn:0,11 Col.:0 Hsr.:4,12

Quantity of ingredients:
Oat flakes (whole grain) 1 cup / 125g. (yes)
Walnuts 1 table spoon / 15g. (rec.)
Hazelnuts 1 table spoon / 15g. (yes)
Water 1 1/2 cups / 240g. (yes)
Wakame 1 inch / 2g. (yes)
Apple (sweet) 1 piece / 220g. (yes)
Cardamom 3-4 capsules / 2g. (yes)
Lemon Balm (fresh) 3-4 leaves / 3g. (yes)
Acerola fruit nectar or powder 1 teaspoon / 2g. (yes)

Cooking instructions:
Roast oatmeal and nuts. Add hot water. Add cardamom, wakame and cook for 20 min. Add grated apple, acerola and lemon herb.

9.21 Oriental rice pan

Forcing spleen, dissolves stagnation, promotes weight loss. Good to fight immunodeficiency, loss of appetite, flatulence, high blood pressure, helps to digest fat, strengthens kidney and bladder.
Numerous vitamins, minerals and secondary plant active ingredients.
Cooking time approx. 30 min
Allergens: EL
6 portions to 271,83g. / 303kcal. - (carb:81% / prot:19%)
100g.=111,47kcal. / protein 9,51g. fat:5,44g.
µg. - Ph:2,35 Na:0,71 Ka:4,97 Mg:1,97 Ca:4,24 Fe:0,03 Zn:0,01 Col.:0 Hsr.:2,04

Quantity of ingredients:
Rice (whole grain) 3/8 lbs - 6oz / 180g. (yes)
Basic recipe for a vegetable soup (nutritious) 2 1/4 cups / 500g. (yes)
Curry 1/2 teaspoon / 2g. (yes)
Onion (spring onion) 4 pieces / 80g. (yes)
Rapeseed oil 2 table spoons / 20g. (rec.)
Peppers 1/4 lbs - 4oz / 120g. (rec.)

Corn 3 oz / 80g. (yes)
Shiitake, dried 1/2 oz / 80g. (yes)
Bamboo shoots 3 oz / 80g. (yes)
Peas 3 oz / 80g. (yes)
Peaches 1/8 lbs - 2oz / 60g. (yes)
Pineapple 1/8 lbs - 2oz / 60g. (yes)
Tomato 5/8 oz / 200g. (yes)
Lovage 1 teaspoon / 2g. (yes)
Basil (fresh) 1 teaspoon / 2g. (yes)
Parsley 1 teaspoon / 2g. (yes)
Lemon Balm (fresh) 1 teaspoon / 2g. (yes)
Pepper (ground) 1 pinch / 1g. ()

Cooking instructions:
Soak the mushrooms in water 20 min.
Boil the rice in the vegetable stock 15 min. and season with some curry.
Peel the onion, cut into fine cubes.
Heat the oil in a pan and sauté the onion cubes.
Wash the peppers in half, remove the core, cut into cubes and add.
Add corn, mushrooms and bamboo shoots, simmer 5 min. until firm.
Also add the bean sprouts, peas, peach cubes and pineapple cubes.
Then add the peeled, chopped tomatoes.
Add the cooked rice and season with the herbs and pepper.

9.22 Plum Cake

Cancer preventive effect, dehydrates the body, stimulates digestion and binds fats in the intestine, good to fight loss of appetite, flatulence, inflammatory bowel disease, obesity, gout, stomach ulcers, stomach cramps, rheumatism, heartburn. Relieves pain, detoxifying, bactericide.
Cooking time approx. 1 hour
Allergens: AG
6 portions to 307,83g. / 502kcal. - (carb:71% / prot:29%)
100g.=163,24kcal. / protein 12,32g. fat:19,28g.
µg. - Ph:2,65 Na:0,77 Ka:5,44 Mg:0,5 Ca:0,87 Fe:0,03 Zn:0,02 Col.:0,05 Hsr.:1,38

Quantity of ingredients:
Curd cheese 20% 5/8 oz / 200g. (yes)
Wheat flour 7/8 lbs / 400g. (yes)
Cow's milk (whole milk 3.5% fat) 6 table spoons / 70g. (little)
Rapeseed oil 6 table spoons / 70g. (rec.)

Honey 8 table spoons / 100g. (yes)
Baking powder 1 package / 3g. (yes)
Salt 1 pinch / 1g. (little)
Cinnamon ground 1 teaspoon / 3g. (yes)
Plums 2,2 lbs / 1000g. (yes)

Cooking instructions:
Mix the flour, curd cheese, milk, oil, honey, salt and baking powder into a smooth dough. Keep the dough cool for 15 minutes to cool.
Lay out baking paper on a baking sheet and press the dough out to a bottom.
Now spread the plums evenly.
Sprinkle the cake with the cinnamon and bake for about 40 minutes at 190 ° C/374 °F.

9.23 Provencal noodle pan

Improves blood circulation, reduces Inflammation, relieves pain, strengthens the muscles, tendons and bones, diuretic, supports urination.
Cooking time approx. 45 min
Allergens: ACL
2 portions to 283,5g. / 196kcal. - (carb:62% / prot:38%)
100g.=68,96kcal. / protein 12,83g. fat:4,7g.
µg. - Ph:24,21 Na:3,49 Ka:42,72 Mg:11,18 Ca:16,82 Fe:0,37 Zn:0,31 Col.:1,61 Hsr.:24,25

Quantity of ingredients:
Noodles (whole grain) with egg 5/8 oz / 200g. (little)
Aubergine 1/8 lbs - 2oz / 60g. (yes)
Zucchini 1/8 lbs - 2oz / 60g. (yes)
Peppers 1/8 lbs - 2oz / 50g. (rec.)
Beef meat 1/8 lbs - 2oz / 50g. (little)
Garlic 2 pieces / 4g. (yes)
Rapeseed oil 1/8 oz / 5g. (rec.)
Basic recipe for a vegetable soup (nutritious) 1/4 cup / 60g. (yes)
Tomato juice 1/3 cup / 75g. (yes)
Oregano fresh 1 pinch / 1g. (yes)
Rosemary 1 pinch / 1g. (yes)
Pepper (ground) 1 pinch / 0,5g. ()
Salt 1 pinch / 0,5g. (little)

Cooking instructions:
Boil noodles in plenty of salted water, chill and drain.
Wash vegetables, dice aubergine and zucchini.
Core the pepper and cut into cubes of approx. 1 cm.
Braise garlic, minced beef and prepared vegetables in heated oil, pour in vegetable stock and tomato juice and finish cooking.
Add pasta to the sauce.
Heat the whole and season with the spices and salt.

9.24 Pumpkin-yoghurt soup

Relaxes, reduces blood pressure, strengthens immune system, promotes weight loss. Good to fight immunodeficiency, loss of appetite, flatulence, depressions, diabetes, diarrhea.
Cooking time approx. 15 min
Allergens: GL
4 portions to 239g. / 68kcal. - (carb:83% / prot:17%)
100g.=28,45kcal. / protein 2,37g. fat:1,31g.
μg. - Ph:1,79 Na:0,9 Ka:6,6 Mg:2,8 Ca:10,96 Fe:0,02 Zn:0,01 Col.:0,05 Hsr.:0,35

Quantity of ingredients:
Basic recipe for a vegetable soup (nutritious) 1 cup / 300g. (yes)
Hokkaido pumpkin 1,1 lbs / 500g. (yes)
Ginger fresh 1/2 teaspoon / 2g. (yes)
Fennel seeds ground 1/2 teaspoon / 1g. (yes)
Anise (Common Fennel) 1/4 teaspoon / 1g. (yes)
Yogurt (natural, 1.5% fat) 3/8 lbs - 6oz / 150g. (yes)
Peppermint 2 leaves / 1g. (yes)
Salt 1 pinch / 1g. (little)

Cooking instructions:
Heat the vegetable broth (after the basic recipe) till it boils. Add diced pumpkin, chopped ginger, crushed fennel seeds and anise. Bring the soup to the boil and simmer for about 12 minutes until the pumpkin is soft.
Remove soup from the heat. Puree the soup with the yoghurt with the blender. Serve soup with finely chopped mint sprinkled.

9.25 Quick flakes with compote or jam

Relieves pain, detoxifying, bactericide. Dissolves stones. Promotes digestion, nourishes bones and tendons, warms kidneys and spleen, forcing spleen, neutralizes Flatulence, controls excessive urge to urinate, helps to fight digestive weakness.

Cooking time approx. 5 min

Allergens: H

2 portions to 219g. / 189kcal. - (carb:64% / prot:36%)
100g.=86,3kcal. / protein 4,12g. fat:8,82g.
µg. - Ph:2,17 Na:0,24 Ka:3,41 Mg:0,86 Ca:1,28 Fe:0,03 Zn:0,03 Col.:0 Hsr.:0,14

Quantity of ingredients:

Quinoa 5-7 table spoons / 50g. (yes)
Water 1 cup / 250g. (yes)
Compote (fruits of the season) 1 cup / 100g. (yes)
Walnuts 1 table spoon (grated) / 8g. (rec.)
Olive oil 1 table spoon / 10g. (yes)
Honey 2 table spoons / 20g. (yes)
Vanilla 1 pinch / 0,2g. (yes)
Anise (Common Fennel) 1 pinch / 0,2g. (yes)
Cardamom 1 pinch / 0,2g. (yes)
Chili (pod or ground) 1 pinch / 0,1g. (yes)

Cooking instructions:

Put the quinoa flakes in a pan and add water. Boil for 3-5 minutes, pull from the fire, add nuts and compote. Add a dash of oil. Sweeten as needed with honey, whole cane sugar or agave syrup.

Spices and aromas: vanilla, anise, fennel or coriander, cardamom, a little chili.

Winter: apple compote, pear compote, fruit jam.

Summer: plum compote, apricot compote.

9.26 Rhubarb cake with sprinkles

Laxative, antipyretic. Protects the digestive system. Detoxifying, affects anorexia, good to fight flatulence, inflammatory bowel disease, brittle nails and hair. Relieves pain, detoxifying, against dry skin, acne, eczema.

Cooking time approx. 1 1/2 hours

Allergens: AG

8 portions to 239,5g. / 476kcal. - (carb:72% / prot:28%)
100g.=198,64kcal. / protein 12,39g. fat:15,41g.
µg. - Ph:1,84 Na:0,16 Ka:3,72 Mg:0,47 Ca:0,65 Fe:0,03 Zn:0,02 Col.:0,01 Hsr.:1,51

Quantity of ingredients:
Wheat flour 7/8 lbs / 400g. (yes)
Cow's milk (whole milk 3.5% fat) 1 cup / 200g. (little)
Yeast 1 oz / 30g. (yes)
Honey 2 teaspoons / 5g. (yes)
Sunflower oil 2 teaspoons / 5g. (yes)
Lemon peel 1 piece / 3g. (yes)
Salt 1 pinch / 1g. (little)
Rhubarb 2,2 lbs / 800g. (yes)
Margarine 1/4 lbs - 4oz / 120g. (yes)
Wheat flour 3/4 lbs / 300g. (yes)
Vanilla sugar natural 2 pinches / 1g. (yes)
Cinnamon ground 2 pinches / 1g. (yes)
Honey 5 table spoons / 50g. (yes)

Cooking instructions:
Mix flour, grated lemon peel and salt.
Heat milk gently and mix with yeast and honey.
Then add the flour mixture and the oil and knead vigorously. Cover the dough and let it rise in a warm place until it reaches twice the amount. (about 30 minutes)

For the sprinkles, mix flour with vanilla and cinnamon, then add honey and margarine and crumble to a crumbly mass. Keep the sprinkles dough cool.

Lay out a baking sheet with parchment paper.
Knead the dough for the bottom again, roll it out, place it on the baking sheet and let it rise for another 10 minutes.

Clean the rhubarb, wash it, halve lengthwise and cut into pieces of approx. 3 cm. Spread the pieces on the rolled out dough and crumble the sprinkles over the cake.

Place the cake in the preheated oven at 175 ° C and bake for about 40 minutes.

9.27 Rice congee with crushed walnuts

Good to fight blood circulation disorders, high blood pressure, a headache, for the drainage of the body overweight and high blood pressure. Dissolves stones. Warms stomach and spleen, improves blood circulation. Antipyretic.

Cooking time approx. 2 hours and more

Allergens: H

2 portions to 295g. / 406kcal. - (carb:82% / prot:18%)
100g.=137,8kcal. / protein 7,9g. fat:22,82g.
µg. - Ph:15,8 Na:0,24 Ka:17,23 Mg:68,48 Ca:64,13 Fe:0,14 Zn:0,12 Col.:0 Hsr.:2,22

Quantity of ingredients:
Basic recipe for a rice soup (Congee) 4 cups / 500g. (yes)
Sugar cane sugar 2 table spoons / 20g. (little)
Walnuts 1 cup / 70g. (rec.)
Cinnamon ground 1 pinch / 0,2g. (yes)

Cooking instructions:
Cook the basic recipe for rice soup (congee)
Note: The crushed walnuts can be cooked from the beginning.
Variation: Refine with sweet or spicy ingredients as you like. In particular, cinnamon, cloves, and ginger increase the warming effect and wholesomeness.

9.28 Roasted nuts

Dissolves stones. Good to fight depressions. Strengths spleen and stomach.

Cooking time approx. 5 min

Allergens: H

2 portions to 150g. / 973kcal. - (carb:17% / prot:83%)
100g.=648,67kcal. / protein 22,6g. fat:85,5g.
µg. - Ph:97,58 Na:1,75 Ka:142,42 Mg:45 Ca:29,42 Fe:0,87 Zn:0,78 Col.:0 Hsr.:5,83

Quantity of ingredients:
Hazelnuts 1/4 lbs - 4oz / 100g. (yes)
Cashews 1/4 lbs - 4oz / 100g. (yes)
Walnuts 1/4 lbs - 4oz / 100g. (rec.)

Cooking instructions:
Roast nuts in a pan for about 5 minutes.

9.29 Salmon on tomato-spinach

Promotes bowel movement, improves blood circulation, forcing spleen and bowel, strengthens blood, reduces inflammation, improves digestion, regenerates skin, supports urination, lowers cholesterol, promotes sweating, dissolves stagnation.
Cooking time approx. 1 hour
Allergens: D
6 portions to 354,5g. / 365kcal. - (carb:27% / prot:73%)
100g.=102,87kcal. / protein 29,53g. fat:29,9g.
µg. - Ph:3,21 Na:1,24 Ka:8,91 Mg:0,84 Ca:1,38 Fe:0,04 Zn:0,01 Col.:0,28 Hsr.:2,03

Quantity of ingredients:
Potato 1,1 lbs / 500g. (yes)
Salt 1 pinch / 1g. (little)
Salmon 1,3 lbs / 600g. (rec.)
Rapeseed oil 2 teaspoons / 24g. (rec.)
Tomato 1/4 lbs - 4oz / 100g. (yes)
Spinach 1,5 lbs / 700g. (yes)
Salt 1 pinch / 1g. (little)
Pine nuts 4 table spoons / 40g. (yes)
Leek 1/4 lbs - 4oz / 120g. (yes)
Olive oil 4 table spoons / 40g. (yes)
Salt 1 pinch / 1g. (little)
Pepper white (ground) 1 pinch / 0,5g. (yes)

Cooking instructions:
Peel the potato and cut into cubes, cook in salted water.
Cut the salmon into portions and fry slowly and evenly in a frying pan from both sides, seasoned with salt and pepper, then add the pine nuts and lightly roast.
Blanch spinach in salted water.
Lightly sweat the finely chopped leek with a little rapeseed oil, add the blanched spinach and heat evenly.
Just before serving, add the halved cocktail tomatoes to the spinach and season the vegetables well with salt and pepper.
Arrange the spinach and leek tomato bed with the potatoes, add the salmon and sprinkle with the salted pine nuts.

Drizzle with a little olive oil and serve the dish.

9.30 Semolina dumpling with mascarpone

Relieves pain and inflammation, little laxative. Protects the digestive system. Detoxifying, affects anorexia, good to fight flatulence, inflammatory bowel disease, obesity, gout, stomach ulcers, stomach cramps, rheumatism, heartburn, twelffinger intestinal ulcers.
Cooking time approx. 25 min

Allergens: AG

3 portions to 355g. / 331kcal. - (carb:62% / prot:38%)
100g.=93,33kcal. / protein 9,72g. fat:14,94g.
µg. - Ph:7,34 Na:2,6 Ka:15,7 Mg:1,52 Ca:7,48 Fe:0,08 Zn:0,03 Col.:0,51 Hsr.:2,62

Quantity of ingredients:
Cow's milk (1.5% fat) 1 1/2 cups / 400g. (yes)
Wheat semolina 0,2 lbs / 70g. (yes)
Cinnamon ground 1 pinch / 0,5g. (yes)
Lemon peel 1 pinch / 1g. (yes)
Honey 1 teaspoon / 3g. (yes)
Vanilla pod 1 pinch / 0,5g. (yes)
Mascarpone cheese 3 oz / 80g. ()
Strawberries 1,1 lbs / 500g. (yes)
Honey 1 table spoon / 10g. (yes)

Cooking instructions:
In a small saucepan, heat the milk till it boil while stirring. Stir in semolina, cinnamon and lemon peel and cook 6 minutes stirring until thick, firm paste.

Mix the semolina, honey, vanilla and mascarpone into a smooth mixture with the hand mixer. Allow the mass to cool
in the refrigerator.

For the sauce, puree strawberries with honey in a blender.
Spread a few spoons of fruit sauce on a large plate. With 2 tablespoons, cut off dumplings from the semolina mass (to prevent sticking, rinse in cold water again and again). Put the dumplings on the fruit sauce.
It looks especially nice when the dessert is still garnished with a few berries and herbal leaves.

9.31 Semolina soup with vegetables

Reduces blood pressure, strengthens immune system, prevents cancer, forcing spleen, dissolves stagnation, promotes weight loss. Good to fight immunodeficiency, loss of appetite, flatulence, high blood pressure, depressions, diabetes, diarrhea, rheumatism, heartburn, twelffinger intestinal ulcers.
Cooking time approx. 20 min
Allergens: AGL
3 portions to 237,67g. / 105kcal. - (carb:85% / prot:15%)
100g.=44,32kcal. / protein 2,38g. fat:4,24g.
µg. - Ph:2,88 Na:3,04 Ka:8,54 Mg:9,5 Ca:37,49 Fe:0,11 Zn:0,03 Col.:0 Hsr.:1,7

Quantity of ingredients:
Basic recipe for a vegetable soup (nutritious) 2 cup / 500g. (yes)
Wheat semolina 2 table spoons / 20g. (yes)
Lovage 1/2 teaspoon / 2g. (yes)
Basil (fresh) 1/2 teaspoon / 1g. (yes)
Nutmeg 1 pinch / 0,1g. (yes)
Carrot 1/4 lbs - 4oz / 100g. (yes)
Celery root 1/8 lbs - 2oz / 50g. (yes)
Cream, sweet 30% 3 table spoons / 30g. (little)
Parsley 1 table spoon / 10g. (yes)

Cooking instructions:
Roast wheat grits without fat in a pan. Roast the chopped carrots and celery briefly. Add the vegetable soup (Basic recipe for a vegetable soup). Season with lovage, nutmeg and let it 10 min. simmer.
Stir in the cream before serving and garnish with parsley.

9.32 Spelled with fruit and nuts

Stops diarrhea, promotes digestion, appetizing, relieves fatigue, anti-inflammatory (gastrointestinal). Good to fight tumor lesions and leukemia, is antiallergic in food allergies, regulates metabolism, lowers blood glucose and cholesterol.
Cooking time approx. 1 1/2 hours
Allergens: AH
3 portions to 286,33g. / 290kcal. - (carb:76% / prot:24%)
100g.=101,16kcal. / protein 8,64g. fat:6,67g.
µg. - Ph:9,7 Na:8,81 Ka:25,53 Mg:3,53 Ca:2,83 Fe:0,14 Zn:0,02 Col.:0 Hsr.:2,96

Quantity of ingredients:
Spelled grain 1 cup / 120g. (yes)
Water 1 cup / 50g. (yes)
Apple (sweet) 1 piece / 220g. (yes)
Apricot 1 piece / 200g. (yes)
Peaches 1 piece / 120g. (yes)
Cinnamon ground 1 pinch / 1g. (yes)
Cardamom 1 pinch / 1g. (yes)
Salt 1 pinch / 1g. (little)
Strawberries 1 cup / 120g. (yes)
Almond puree 1 table spoon / 15g. (yes)
Cocoa 1 pinch / 1g. (yes)
Walnuts 1 table spoon / 10g. (rec.)

Cooking instructions:
Put spelled in hot water and cook.

Then: Give sweet chopped fruit (apples, apricots, peaches) in a little hot water, with a little cinnamon, sauté briefly; ground cardamom and / or coriander, a small pinch of salt, the boiled spelled, berries after season. Put some cocoa and roasted nuts over it.

9.33 Spicy cake with dates

Good to fight loss of appetite, flatulence, inflammatory bowel disease, obesity, gout, stomach ulcers, stomach cramps, rheumatism, heartburn. Calms nerves and stomach, improves blood circulation.
Cooking time approx. 1 1/2 hours
Allergens: ACGO
4 portions to 232,5g. / 808kcal. - (carb:71% / prot:29%)
100g.=347,31kcal. / protein 14,11g. fat:32,9g.
µg. - Ph:9,62 Na:3,38 Ka:13,75 Mg:2,43 Ca:2,59 Fe:0,12 Zn:0,07 Col.:4,87 Hsr.:3,22

Quantity of ingredients:
Sunflower oil 1/2 cup / 100g. (yes)
Sugar white 5/8 oz / 200g. (little)
Cow's milk (whole milk 3.5% fat) 1/2 cup / 100g. (little)
Wheat flour 5/8 lbs - 8oz / 250g. (yes)
Cocoa 1/8 lbs - 2oz / 40g. (yes)
Dates dried 1/8 lbs - 2oz / 50g. (yes)
Chicken egg 3 pieces / 180g. (little)
Clove 1/2 teaspoon / 1g. (yes)

Cinnamon ground 1 1/2 tea spoon / 3g. (yes)
Nutmeg 1 pinch / 0,5g. (yes)
Baking powder 1/2 package / 1,5g. (yes)
Butter organic 1 teaspoon / 2g. (little)
Wheat flour 1 teaspoon / 2g. (yes)

Cooking instructions:

Separate eggs. Stir egg whites until stiff and set aside.
Add oil, sugar, egg yolk to a bowl and stir until frothy.
Add the flour, cocoa and baking powder, stir. Stir in the milk. Now add
the minced dates and the spices (the cloves
as grated powder) to the mixture and mix with low speed of the hand
mixer.
Now, take the stiffly egg white spoonful carefully under.
Put the dough in a greased, floured mold and bake at 200°C/392°F for
70 minutes.

9.34 Spring salad

Blood-forming, blood detoxifying, diuretic, good to fight stomach
discomfort, improves digestion, diarrhea, helps to digest fat, supports
urination, reduces blood pressure, detoxifying, reduces inflammation,
diuretic.
Cooking time approx. 10 min
Allergens: AEMNO
4 portions to 214,25g. / 180kcal. - (carb:64% / prot:36%)
100g.=84,13kcal. / protein 7,68g. fat:5,56g.
µg. - Ph:14,38 Na:19,94 Ka:78,76 Mg:7,01 Ca:20,61 Fe:0,72 Zn:0,03 Col.:0 Hsr.:7,87

Quantity of ingredients:

Sorrel 3/8 lbs - 6oz / 150g. (yes)
Dandelion (young plants) 1/4 lbs - 4oz / 100g. (yes)
Mung bean sprouting 0,2 lbs / 75g. (yes)
Cress 1/4 lbs - 4oz / 100g. (yes)
Chives 1 Bunch / 50g. (yes)
Tomato 2 pieces / 100g. (yes)
Parsley 1 Bunch / 50g. (yes)
Sesame paste (Tahini) 2 table spoons / 16g. (yes)
Soy sauce 1 dash / 3g. (yes)
Mustard 1/2 teaspoon / 2g. (rec.)
White bread (wheat bread) 6 slices / 120g. (yes)
Vinegar Aceto Balsamico 1 table spoon / 8g. (yes)
Olive oil 1 table spoon / 8g. (yes)

Cooking instructions:
Wash all salad´s, mix and prepare the sauce as follows:
Mix tahini with mustard and balsamic vinegar, tamari, olive oil, chives and half of parsley. Pour the sauce over the salad and sprinkle the remaining parsley just before serving.
Serve with the white bread.

9.35 Sweet potato pancakes with basil pesto

Strengthens the immune system, reduces fat, improves digestion, calms nerves and stomach, dissolves stones, improves blood circulation, strengthens the muscles, antioxidative.
Cooking time approx. 30 min
Allergens: ACH
3 portions to 298,67g. / 625kcal. - (carb:58% / prot:42%)
100g.=209,26kcal. / protein 15,5g. fat:32,67g.
µg. - Ph:14,41 Na:8,52 Ka:39,8 Mg:4,23 Ca:5,79 Fe:0,17 Zn:0,11 Col.:6,88 Hsr.:2,11

Quantity of ingredients:
Sweet potato 4 pieces / 500g. (yes)
Onion read 1/2 piece / 30g. (yes)
Basil 1 table spoon / 10g. (yes)
Chicken egg 2 pieces / 140g. (little)
Spelled wholemeal flour 3 oz / 80g. (yes)
Salt 1 pinch / 0,5g. (little)
Olive oil 1/4 cup / 20g. (yes)
Salt 1 teaspoon (coarse) / 3g. (little)
Basil 1 handful / 15g. (yes)
Parsley 1 handful / 15g. (yes)
Garlic 2 cloves / 3g. (yes)
Walnuts 1/8 lbs - 2oz / 60g. (rec.)
Olive oil 2 table spoons / 20g. (yes)

Cooking instructions:
Sweet Potato Buffer: Wash the sweet potato thoroughly, but do not peel, and grate into a large bowl. Add onion, basil, egg and flour, mix well and sprinkle with salt. The mixture can be formed into buffers. Bake in a preheated tube on a baking tray coated with oil for 4 to 5 minutes on both sides.

Basil Pesto: Add the salt, chopped basil and parsley and crushed garlic in a small bowl and crush (if available, use the mortar). Add the grated walnuts. While stirring, add enough olive oil until the desired consistency is achieved.

9.36 Szeged fishbowl

Promotes spleen, stomach and kidneys, improves digestion, dissolves stagnation, reduces blood pressure, strengthens immune system.
Cooking time approx. 30 min
Allergens: ADL
2 portions to 380,5g. / 280kcal. - (carb:58% / prot:42%)
100g.=73,59kcal. / protein 25,32g. fat:3,09g.
µg. - Ph:25,89 Na:22,72 Ka:60,47 Mg:11,78 Ca:30,28 Fe:0,18 Zn:0,12 Col.:4,99 Hsr.:13,6

Quantity of ingredients:
Cod 5/8 oz / 200g. (rec.)
Lemon 1/4 piece / 5g. (yes)
Pork Bacon 1/8 lbs - 2oz / 40g. (little)
Onion (spring onion) 2 pieces / 40g. (yes)
Sauerkraut (cutted cabbage fermented) 5/8 lbs - 8oz / 250g. (yes)
Tomato paste 2 table spoons / 20g. (yes)
Basic recipe for a vegetable soup (nutritious) 1/2 cup / 150g. (yes)
Salt 1 pinch / 1g. (little)
Peppers powder 1 pinch / 1g. (yes)
Ground caraway 1 pinch / 1g. (yes)
Pepper (ground) 1 pinch / 0,5g. ()
Spelled wholemeal flour 1 teaspoon / 3g. (yes)
Bread with carob kernel flour 2 slices / 50g. (yes)

Cooking instructions:
Clean the fish fillets, sprinkle with lemon, salt.
Roast the bacon in a deep, large pan. Add the finely chopped onions and roast for a short time. Add sauerkraut and tomato paste. Fill with vegetable stock and stew for about 10 to 15 minutes with the lid closed.
Put prepared fish cubes on the sauerkraut. Season with paprika, caraway, pepper and simmer for about 10 minutes over low heat.
Tie with some flour or cornstarch.
Serve with bread.

9.37 Tea from birch leaves

This tea is diuretic and helps to fight kidney problems, gout, also helps with bacterial and inflammatory urinary tract diseases, rheumatic complaints.
Cooking time approx. 10 min
4 portions to 126,25g. / 0kcal. - (carb:0% / prot:0%)
100g.=0kcal. / protein 0g. fat:0g.
µg. - Ph:0 Na:0,06 Ka:0 Mg:0,06 Ca:0,31 Fe:0 Zn:0,01 Col.:0 Hsr.:0

Quantity of ingredients:
Water 2 cup / 500g. (yes)

Cooking instructions:
Brew birch leaves with boiling water, let stand for 10 minutes, drink 1 cup 3 times a day.

9.38 Tea from elderberry blossom tea

Good, if you have a sore throat. Good to fight colds. Promotes urination, good to fight flu, urinary stones, concentration weakness, blackheads, hay fever, rheumatism. Strengthen the immune system, diaphoretic.
Cooking time approx. 10 min
4 portions to 128g. / 7kcal. - (carb:0% / prot:0%)
100g.=5,47kcal. / protein 0g. fat:0g.
µg. - Ph:0 Na:0,06 Ka:0 Mg:0,06 Ca:0,3 Fe:0 Zn:0,01 Col.:0 Hsr.:0

Quantity of ingredients:
Elderberry blossom tee 4 teaspoons / 12g. (rec.)
Water 2 cup / 500g. (yes)

Cooking instructions:
Heat the water till it boils and put it aside. Add elderberry blossom tea and 10 min. to let go. Sweet to taste with honey. Strain when pouring.

9.39 Tea from Melissa

Calming effect, good to fight sleep disorders, restlessness and stomach discomfort, allergies, asthma, migraine and bloating, headache, rheumatism. For strengthening after cold and infectious diseases.
Cooking time approx. 10 min
4 portions to 126g. / 0kcal. - (carb:0% / prot:0%)
100g.=0kcal. / protein 0g. fat:0g.
µg. - Ph:0 Na:0,06 Ka:0 Mg:0,06 Ca:0,31 Fe:0 Zn:0,01 Col.:0 Hsr.:0

Quantity of ingredients:
Balm 2 teaspoons / 4g. (yes)
Water 2 cup / 500g. (yes)

Cooking instructions:
Heat the water till it boils and put it aside. Add lemon balm and 10 min. to let go. Sweet to taste with honey. Strain when pouring.

9.40 Tea rooibos

Antioxidant, anti-inflammatory, anticancer, flavonoids, it also has a positive effect on Alzheimer, arteriosclerosis. Antiallergic, inhibits histamine release. Antibacterial, antiviral, antifungal, detoxifying.
Cooking time approx. 10 min.
5 portions to 200,8g. / 0kcal. - (carb:0% / prot:0%)
100g.=0kcal. / protein 0g. fat:0g.
µg. - Ph:0 Na:0,2 Ka:0 Mg:0,2 Ca:1 Fe:0 Zn:0,02 Col.:0 Hsr.:0

Quantity of ingredients:
Rooibos tea 4 teaspoons / 4g. (rec.)
Water 4 cup / 1000g. (yes)

Cooking instructions:
Brew 3-4 teaspoons of rooibos with one liter of boiling water and leave for 6-10 minutes. With soft water you use less tea for the preparation, with harder water we recommend a higher dosage.

9.41 Turkey breast with vegetables (Asian)

Strengthens blood, strengthens bone marrow, dissolves stagnation, promotes digestion and is goo to fight high blood pressure. Rice to drain the body at overweight and high blood pressure.
Cooking time approx. 45 min
Allergens: AEN
2 portions to 371g. / 535kcal. - (carb:54% / prot:46%)
100g.=144,2kcal. / protein 31,92g. fat:18,02g.
µg. - Ph:27,73 Na:66,82 Ka:46,74 Mg:7,57 Ca:3,14 Fe:0,2 Zn:0,21 Col.:4,05 Hsr.:15,18

Quantity of ingredients:
Rice variety any 1 cup / 120g. (yes)
Water 6 cups / 240g. (yes)
Turkey breast meat 5/8 oz / 200g. (yes)
Ginger fresh 1/3 inch / 3g. (yes)
Garlic 1 piece / 2g. (yes)
Soy sauce 2 table spoons / 20g. (yes)
Wheat flour 2 teaspoons / 15g. (yes)
Onion (spring onion) 2 pieces / 40g. (yes)
Peppers 1/2 piece / 10g. (rec.)
Champignon 8 pieces / 30g. (yes)
Sesame oil 2 table spoons / 20g. (yes)
Soy sauce 1 table spoon / 12g. (yes)
Curry 1 pinch / 2g. (yes)
Turmeric (yellow root) 1 pinch / 2g. (yes)

Chili (pod or ground) 1 pinch / 1g. (yes)
Cashews 2 teaspoons / 25g. (yes)

Cooking instructions:
Cook the rice in salted water.
Cut the turkey meat into thin strips. Peel and dice the ginger and garlic.
Put together with the meat strips in a bowl. Mix 1 tbsp of soy sauce with
the wheat starch and stir until smooth. Add to the meat and marinate for
30 minutes. Wash spring onions and peppers, clean and cut into small
pieces. Clean and quarter the mushrooms.
Put one tablespoon of sesame oil in a pan and sauté and warm the
marinated turkey. Now add the remaining oil to the pan and fry the other
vegetables in it. Now add the meat and season with soy sauce and
spices. Serve with the rice. Sprinkle the cashews over the dish before
serving.

9.42 Vegetarian vegetable-oatmeal-potatoes mash

Improves digestion, regenerates skin, supports urination, lowers
cholesterol, supports urination, relieves constipation.
Cooking time approx. 25 min
Allergens: A
2 portions to 109g. / 91kcal. - (carb:61% / prot:39%)
100g.=83,49kcal. / protein 1,89g. fat:4,42g.
µg. - Ph:13,11 Na:2,56 Ka:62,42 Mg:5,72 Ca:8,05 Fe:0,26 Zn:0,13 Col.:0 Hsr.:5,15

Quantity of ingredients:
Carrot (Early Carrot) 1 oz / 30g. (yes)
Parsnip 1 oz / 30g. (yes)
Zucchini 1 oz / 30g. (yes)
Fennel 1/2 oz / 10g. (yes)
Potato 1/8 lbs - 2oz / 50g. (yes)
Water 1/2 oz / 20g. (yes)
Oat flakes (whole grain) 1/2 oz / 10g. (yes)
Orange juice 1 oz / 30g. (yes)
Rapeseed oil 1/4 oz / 8g. (rec.)

Cooking instructions:
Wash the vegetables and potatoes, dice and fry in a little water. Add
water and oatmeal, puree everything and finally add the oil. Note: This
porridge replaces the vegetable-potato-meat porridge when meat is to
be dispensed with in the infant's diet. Since meat is the best food
source for iron, a vegetarian diet must pay particular attention to a
sufficient supply of iron.

9.43 Warming porridge

Strengthens immune system. Diuretic and laxative. Provides vitamin C.
Dissolves stones. Promotes digestion, detoxifying, promotes
perspiration, reduces blood lipids, stimulates, dissolves stagnation.
Cooking time approx. 10 min
Allergens: AHO
1 portion to 214g. / 357kcal. - (carb:73% / prot:27%)
100g.=166,82kcal. / protein 8,85g. fat:11,41g.
µg. - Ph:135,11 Na:3,26 Ka:194,64 Mg:50,8 Ca:38,34 Fe:1,57 Zn:1,38 Col.:0 Hsr.:47,66

Quantity of ingredients:
Oat flakes (whole grain) 6 table spoons / 60g. (yes)
Fig dried 3 pieces / 15g. (yes)
Star anise 1 piece / 1g. (yes)
Ginger fresh 1 pinch / 0,5g. (yes)
Water 1 cup / 120g. (yes)
Maple syrup 1 table spoon / 10g. (yes)
Walnuts 1 table spoon (chopped) / 8g. (rec.)

Cooking instructions:
Soak the dried fruit. Roast Oatmeal dry. Add dried ginger, star anise or
cinnamon, a little grated ginger and boil everything with water to a
mash. With maple syrup sweet. Whip grated walnuts and sprinkle
before serving.

Effect: Suitable for the cold season.
Caution: Fresh ginger does not drink over a long period of time.

9.44 Yogurt with honey and nuts

Relieves pain, detoxifying, promotes wound healing. Good to fight acute
or chronic constipation of the intestine. Dissolves stones.
Cooking time approx. 5 min
Allergens: GH
1 portion to 167g. / 258kcal. - (carb:61% / prot:39%)
100g.=154,49kcal. / protein 6,79g. fat:12,43g.
µg. - Ph:107,54 Na:38,83 Ka:167,29 Mg:19,4 Ca:104,46 Fe:0,49 Zn:0,54 Col.:10,48
Hsr.:2,16

Quantity of ingredients:
Yogurt (natural, 3.5% fat) 1/4 lbs - 4oz / 125g. (little)
Honey 2 table spoons / 30g. (yes)
Walnuts 1 table spoon / 12g. (rec.)

Cooking instructions:
Mix yoghurt with honey and finely chopped nuts.

9.45 Zucchini semolina cream soup

Good to fight loss of appetite, reduces blood pressure, promotes weight loss. Good to fight loss of appetite, flatulence, inflammatory bowel disease, rheumatism, heartburn.
Cooking time approx. 25 min
Allergens: AGL
4 portions to 341,75g. / 146kcal. - (carb:78% / prot:22%)
100g.=42,72kcal. / protein 4,02g. fat:7,8g.
µg. - Ph:1,7 Na:0,83 Ka:9,09 Mg:4,88 Ca:18,35 Fe:0,08 Zn:0,02 Col.:0,22 Hsr.:0,82

Quantity of ingredients:
Butter organic 1/2 oz / 20g. (little)
Wheat semolina 2 table spoons / 20g. (yes)
Parsley 1 Bunch / 100g. (yes)
Basic recipe for a vegetable soup (nutritious) 3 1/2 cups / 800g. (yes)
Lovage 1/2 teaspoon / 2g. (yes)
Nutmeg 1 pinch / 0,5g. (yes)
Anise (Common Fennel) 1 pinch / 0,5g. (yes)
Zucchini 7/8 lbs / 400g. (yes)
Ginger fresh 1/2 teaspoon / 1g. (yes)
Crème fraiche cheese 2 table spoons / 20g. (little)
Lemon peel 1/4 piece / 2g. (yes)
Salt 1 pinch / 1g. (little)
Pepper (ground) 1 pinch / 0,5g. ()

Cooking instructions:
Melt the butter in a saucepan, add the semolina and fry briefly while stirring. Add half of the chopped parsley, sauté for a short time, pour vegetable broth according to the basic recipe, season with chopped lovage, nutmeg and anise. Cook the soup without lid lightly for 10 minutes. Add the finely chopped zucchini and the small piece of lemon zest, cook gently for 5 minutes until the zucchini are tender. Remove the lemon peel.
Using the blender, finely puree the soup with the crème fraiche and the remaining parsley.

10 Effects of food

10.1 Use ingredients: recommendable

Acai powder
Bitter Herb liqueur
Cod
Codfish
Cream 10% coffee cream
Eel
Elderberry blossom tee
Fish pieces mixed (fresh water)
Fox nut, gorgon nut, makhana
Fresh cheese from soya
Freshwater fish
Halibut (Flatfish)
Herring
Hibiscus
Kudzu
Lily bulbs

Mackerel
Mascarpone cheese
Mediterranean fish (cod, plaice, haddock, sea eel, mackerel)
Perch
Plaice
Rapeseed oil
Rosefish
Salmon
Soya Cuisine (soy cream)
Soybeans
Soybeans, yellow
Trout
Tuna
Walnuts

10.2 Use ingredients: yes

Acerola fruit nectar or powder
Adzuki beans
Agar agar (kelp)
Agave nectar
Agrimony
Almond
Almond marzipan
Almond milk
Almond puree
Aloe juice
Amaranth
Amaranth Pops
Anchovy / Sardine
Angelica root
Anise (Common Fennel)
Apple (sour)
Apple (sweet)
Apple juice (natural cloudy)
Apple puree
Apricot
Apricot dried
Apricot jam
Apricot nectar
Apricots
Apricots juice
Arrowroot
Artichoke
Asparagus (green or white)
Aubergine
Avocado

Baking powder
Balm
Bamboo shoots
Banana
Banana (cooking banana)
Banchatee (green tea)
barberry
Barley
Barley flour
Barley grass powder
Barley grouts
Barley malt
Barley not peeled
Basic recipe for a rice soup (Congee)
Basic recipe for a vegetable soup (nutritious)
Basil
Basil (fresh)
Batavia
Bay leaf
Bean oil
Beans (green, fresh)
Bearberry leaf
Berries of the season
Berry juice
Bitter Lemon
Bitter orange peel
Black beans
Black caraway
Black fungus mushroom

Black tea
Blackberry dried (unripe fruit)
Blackberry jam
Blackberry leaves
Blackberry´s
Black-eyed peas
Blackthorn (Sloe)
Blue mallow tee
Blueberry
Blueberry dried
Blueberry jam
Blueberry juice
Bocksdorn fruits (Fructus Lycii, Goji,
goji berry dried
Boletus mushroom
Borage
Borage oil
Boxhorn clover seeds
Brazil nuts
Bread roll
Bread with carob kernel flour
Breadcrumbs (wheat bread, bread roll)
Broad beans (thick beans)
Broccoli
Brussels sprouts
Buckbean
Buckwheat
Buckwheat (roasted) Kasha
Buckwheat whole grain
Bulgur (cereals)
Burdock root tea
Bush beans
Butter beans white
Calamari
Cantaloupe
Capers in olive oil
Carambola (Star fruit)
Cardamom
Carob flour, St. john's bread
Carp
Carrot
Carrot (Early Carrot)
Carrot juice without sugar
Cashews
Cauliflower
Caviar
Celery root
Celery sticks
Cereal coffee
Chamomile
Chamomile tea
Champignon
Channa-Dal
Chanterelle

Chard
Chenpi (chinese tangerine bowl)
Cherry
Cherry (sour)
Cherry compote
Cherry juice
Chervil
Chervil dried
Chestnut puree
Chestnuts
Chickpeas
Chickweed
Chicory
Chili (pod or ground)
Chinese cabbage
Chinese pearl barley
Chives
Chlorella (fresh water)
Chrysanthemum blossom tea
Cinnamon ground
Cinnamon sticks
Clementine
Clementines
Clove
Cocoa
Coconut flakes
Coconut grated
Coconut meat
Coconut milk
Coffee
Coix (seeds) YiYi Ren
Cola drink (low calorie)
Compote (fruits of the season)
Coriander
Coriander (fresh)
Corn
Corn (fast polenta)
Corn (roasted)
Corn flour
Corn germ oil
Corn Grease (Polenta)
Corn silk tea
Corn starch
Couscous
Cow's milk (1.5% fat)
Crab
Cranberries
Cranberry
Cranberry
Cranberry jam
Cranberry juice
Cream (30% fat)
Cream sour 10%
Creamer

Cress
Crispbread
Crucian
Cucumber
Cucumber (bitter)
Cucumber (spicy cucumber)
Cumin (Caraway seed)
Curcuma
Curd cheese 20%
Currant (black)
Currant (red)
Currant (white)
Currant jam (black)
Currant jam (red)
Currant juice (black)
Currants (black)
Currants (red)
Curry
Curry paste red
Daisy
Dandelion (young plants)
Dandelion juice
Dandelionroots tea
Dashi
Dates dried
Dates red
Deer meat
Deer meat
Deer's Bones
Dill
Dulse (seaweed)
Dyer's broom herb
Eel smoked
Elderberries
Endive salad
Evening primrose oil
Fennel
Fennel seeds ground
Fennel tea
Fenugreek (Trigonella foenum-graecum)
Fig
Fig dried
Fish innards
Fish remains
Fish sauce
Flounder
Flower pollen
French beans
Freshwater crab
Fructose (glucose)
Fruit mix juice
Fruit tea
Gail plum

Galangal
Garam Masala powder
Garlic
Gelatin white
Gelee Royal
Gentian root
Gentian root tea
Ginger fresh
Ginger oil
Ginger powder
Ginkgo fruit
Ginseng
Ginseng root
Goose blood
Gooseberry
Gourd
Grape juice red
Grape juice white
Grapefruit (Pomelo)
Grapefruit dried peel
Grapefruit juice
Grapes red
Grapes white
Grapeseed oil
Grass carp
Green spelt
Green tea
Greengage
Ground
Ground caraway
Guava
Hawthorn
Hazelnuts
Herbal tea mix
Herbs bitter
Herbs of Provence
Herbs various
Herbs wild
Hibiscus tea
Hijiki
Hokkaido pumpkin
Honey
Hop
Horehound leaves
Horse meat
Hyssop
Iceberg lettuce
Jasmine blossoms tee
Jellyfish
Juniper berry
Kaki plum
Kalmus
Kidney beans (red)
King Solomon's-seal

Kiwi
Kohlrabi
Kombu seaweed (Saccharina japonica)
Kukicha tea
Kumquats
Ladyfingers
Lamb meat
Lamb shoulder
Lamb's lettuce
Lamb's lettuce
Lavender blossoms
Leaf salads (bitter)
Leek
Lemon
Lemon Balm (dried)
Lemon Balm (fresh)
Lemon juice
Lemon peel
Lemongrass
Lentils
Lentils black
Lentils red
Lentils yellow
Lettuce
Licorice root tea
Lima beans
Lime
Lime blossom tea
Linseed
Linseed (crushed)
Linseed oil
Liver smoothing tea
Lobster
Loquate / Japanese medlar
Lotus roots
Lotus seeds
Lovage
Lovage seeds
Luo Han Guo fruit
Lychee
Lychee in Preserved
Lye roll
Mallow (Malva sylvestris) blossom tea
Malt
Mango
Mango juice
Manioc flour
Maple syrup
Mare's milk
Margarine
Margarine (diet)
Marjoram
Medlar
Millet

Millet flakes
Mineral water
Mirabelle plum
Miso
Miso black (fermented)
Miso paste (soy bean paste)
Mixed Pickles
Morel (black, dried)
Morel, dried
Mu Erh Mushroom
Muesli
Mulberry fruit
Mulled Wine Spice
Mullet
Multi-grain bread (gray bread)
Mung bean
Mung bean sprouting
Mussels
Mustard
Mustard Dijon
Mustard medium hot
Mustard seeds
Mustard sweet
Mutton
Mutton
Nasturtium (nose-twister or nose-tweaker)
Nectarine
Nettles
Nori, purple seaweed, red algae
Nutmeg
Oat
Oat flakes (whole grain)
Oat flakes roasted
Oat flour
Oat fusion (baby food)
Oat meal
Oat milk
Octopus
Octopus
Okra
Olive oil
Olives
Olives green
Onion (shallot)
Onion (spring onion)
Onion read
Onion white
Orange
Orange blossom
Orange dried peel
Orange grated peel
Orange jam
Orange juice

Orange peel
Oregano dried
Oregano fresh
Oyster mushroom
Oyster shell powder
Oysters
Palm oil
Papaya
Parsley
Parsley root
Parsnip
Passion blossoms tea
Passion fruit
Peaches
Peaches (canned)
Peanut oil
Pear
Pear juice
Pearl barley
Pearl barley
Peas
Peas, green
Pepper (ground)
Pepper Cayenne
Pepper powder (hot)
Pepper white (ground)
Peppercorns
Peppermint
Peppermint tea
Pepperoni
Pepperoni, red, pitted, halved
Pepperoni, yellow, pitted, halved
Peppers
Peppers (rose peppers)
Peppers (sweet)
Peppers powder
Pickle
Pimento
Pine nuts
Pineapple
Pineapple juice without sugar
Pinto beans speckled
Pistachios
Plum
Plum dried
Plums
Pomegranate
Poppy
Potato
Potato (mealy)
Potato flour
Prickly pear
Processed cheese 12%
Psyllium seed

Pudding powder vanilla
Pumpernickel (dark bread)
Pumpkin
Pumpkin seed oil
Pumpkin seeds
Quince
Quinoa
Rabbit
Rabbit (wild)
Rabbit meat
Radicchio
Radish
Radish (white, green, purple-red)
Radish black
Radish horseradish
Radish leaves
Raisins
Raspberry
Raspberry dried (immature)
Raspberry jam
Raspberry leaf tea
Red beet
Red berry (without sugar)
Red cabbage
Red wine
Reishi mushroom
Rhubarb
Ribworttea
Rice (fragrance)
Rice (Gaoliang / Sorghum)
Rice (whole grain)
Rice Basmati
Rice black
Rice flour
Rice long grain rice
Rice malt
Rice mash
Rice noodles
Rice red
Rice round grain
Rice starch
Rice sticky
Rice sweet
Rice variety any
Rice wild (nature rice)
Romaine lettuce / lettuce salad
Rose blossom tea
Rose hip
Rose hip tea
Rose leaf tea
Rosemary
Rucola
Rusk
Rye

Rye flour
Rye wholemeal bread
Safflower (Dyer's thistle / Hong Hua)
Saffron
Sage
Sago (cereals)
Sake
Salsify
Sauerkraut (cutted cabbage fermented)
Savory
Savoy cabbage / kale
Sea buckthorn
Sea cucumber
Seacrab
Sesame oil
Sesame oil roasted
Sesame paste (Tahini)
Sesame, black
Sesame, white
Shark
Shiitake, dried
Shrimp
Shrimps
Skim milk powder
Slug
Sorrel
Sour cherries
Sourdough
Soy flour
Soy noodles
Soy sauce
Soy Tofu
Soy Tofu smoked
Soybean milk
Soybean oil
Soybeans, black
Soybeans, blacks, fermented
Spelled (Dark) bread
Spelled flakes
Spelled grain
Spelled semolina
Spelled wholemeal flour
Spinach
Spiny lobsters
Spurdog (spiny dogfish, Schillerlocken)
St. Benedict's thistle, blessed thistle,
holy thistle, spotted thistle
Star anise
Stevia (candyleaf, sweetleaf)
Strawberries
Strawberry jam
Strawberry Juice
Sugar fructose - fruit sugar
Sugar glucose - grapes sugar

Sugar Milk Sugar
Sugar substitute (sweetener)
Sunflower oil
Sunflower seeds
Sweet potato
Tabasco
Tangerine
Tarragon (Estragon)
Tea mixture uric acid lowering
Thistle oil
Thyme
Thyme dried
Toast bread (whole grain)
Tomato
Tomato dried
Tomato juice
Tomato paste
Tomato puree
Tonic Water
Topinambur
Trout (smoked)
Truffle
Tsampa (roasted barley flour)
Turkey breast meat
Turkey ham
Turmeric (yellow root)
Turnip
Turnips
Umeboshi paste
Umeboshi plums (Japanese apricots)
Valerian
Vanilla
Vanilla pod
Vanilla powder
Vanilla sugar natural
Vegetable juice
Vinegar (Apple vinegar)
Vinegar (Red wine vinegar)
Vinegar Aceto Balsamico
Vinegar Aceto Balsamico white
Wakame
Walnut oil
Water
Water hot
Watermelon
Wax gourd
Wheat
Wheat bran
Wheat bulgur
Wheat flakes
Wheat flatbread/pita bread
Wheat flour
Wheat flour whole grain
Wheat germ oil

Wheat semolina
Wheat semolina for children
Wheat/Rye/Gray-black bread with yeast
Wheatgrass juice
Wheatgrass powder
White beans
White bread (baguette)
White bread (pretzel sticks)
White bread (roll)
White bread (wheat bread)
White breadcrumbs
White cabbage
White dumpling bread (wheat bread cut into chunks)
Whitefish

Whole grain bread
Wholemeal flour
Wild boar meat
Wild garlic (garlic spinach)
Wild herbs
Wild strawberries
Wormwood herb
Yam root, yam root tuber
Yarrow
Yarrow tea
Yeast
Yew nut
Yogi tea
Yogurt (natural, 1.5% fat)
Zucchini

10.3 Use ingredients: little

Beef bone marrow
Beef fillet
Beef heart
Beef heart (calf)
Beef kidney
Beef liver
Beef lungs (calf)
Beef meat
Beef meat (calf)
Beef meatbones
Beef Oxtail pieces
Beef soup meat
Beef stomach
Beer (alcohol-free)
Beer (alcohol-reduced)
Beer (Pils)
Beer (Top-fermented German dark beer)
Bitter liqueur
Brie cheese
Brown ale
Butter (half fat)
Butter Bio
Buttermilk
Camembert
Campari
Chicken Blood
Chicken egg
Chicken egg white
Chicken heart
Chicken liver
Chicken meat
Chicken stomach
Chicken yolk
Chocolate

Chocolate (Diabetic)
Clarified butter
Coconut fat
Cola drink
Cooking oil
Cottage cheese
Cow's milk (whole milk 3.5% fat)
Cream sour 20%
Cream sour 30%
Cream, sweet 30%
Creme fraiche cheese
Curd cheese 40%
Deer's kidneys
Duck (heart)
Duck (slaughtered)
Ducks egg
Edam cheese
Emmental cheese
Fernet Branca (herbal bitter liqueur)
Feta cheese
Feta cheese
Fresh cheese
Fresh cheese with herbs
Ginseng liqueur
Goat
Goat and sheep's blood
Goat and sheep's brain
Goat and sheep's liver
Goat and sheep's milk
Goat and sheep's stomach
Goat cheese
Goose
Goose egg
Goose fat
Goose parts

Gorgonzola
Gouda cheese
Honey wine (Met)
Kefir
Lamb bones
Lamb kidneys
Lamb liver
Longane
Lychee liqueur
Martini
Mayonnaise 50%
Mayonnaise 80%
Mold cheese
Mozzarella
Noodles (wheat) with egg
Noodles (wheat, lasagne) with egg
Noodles (wheat, ribbon noodles) with egg
Noodles (wheat, spaghetti) with egg
Noodles (whole grain) with egg
Parmesan
Peanut (roasted)
Peanut butter
Peanuts
Pheasant
Pig blood
Pigeon
Pigeon egg
Pineapple (from a can)
Pork Bacon
Pork brain
Pork fat (lard)
Pork ham
Pork ham cooked
Pork ham smoked
Pork heart
Pork kidneys
Pork knuckle
Pork Lard

Pork liver
Pork lung
Pork marrow bones
Pork meat
Pork sausage (Bratwurst)
Pork skin
Pork stomach
Pork/beef sausage (smoked)
Pork's intestine
processed cheese 30%
Prosecco
Puff pastry
Quail
Quail egg
Rabbit liver
Rum
Salt
Salt (herbal)
Sheep's milk
Sheep's milk yoghurt
Sherry (whine)
Sour cream 15% fat
Sour milk
Sour milk cheese 20%
Spirit
Sugar - icing sugar
Sugar brown
Sugar candy white
Sugar cane sugar
Sugar molasses
Sugar palm sugar
Sugar white
Walnuts roasted
Wheat beer
Whey
White wine
Wormwood
Yoghurt vanilla
Yogurt (natural, 3.5% fat)

10.4 Do not use contra-acting foods

Supplementary nutrition

11 Complementary

11.1 Agrimony

Agrimonia eupatoria
Preparation: Healing tea (infusion)
Against persistent rheumatism, bed-wetting, some inflammations in the

mouth, and milkyides.
1-4 g of dried tea as a decoction, 1-4 ml tincture
The herb contains many bitter and tannins and therefore helps as a tea in gastrointestinal diseases and liver disease. As a gargle, however, also relieves gingivitis, sore throat and coughing.

11.2 Angelica (root)

Radix Angelica
Preparation: Decoction
Eliminate pus. Stimulates perspiration and cleansing through the skin, relieves pain and inflammation in rheumatism.
Decoction from 3-6 g, drink in two doses on an empty stomach.

11.3 Arnica (wolf's bane)

Arnica montana, flor.
Preparation: Oil for massage
Arnica massage oil promotes blood circulation, loosens the muscles and protects against unpleasant muscle soreness. Massage oil from 10g Arnika flowers and 50g aloe vera oil and let it stand for 3 weeks (possibly put in the sun and shake occasionally).
Prepare massage oil from 10g arnica blossoms and 50g aloe vera oil and leave to stand for 3 weeks (if necessary put in the sun and shake occasionally).
Arnica blossoms are used in: tissue and organ damage (e.g., mechanical effects and disorders of the blood supply); Injuries such as strains, bruises. After washing, bathing, showering or swimming, massage gently into the still moist skin. During pregnancy use regularly to avoid stretch marks.
It is not recommended to use arnica internally. It can cause nausea, vomiting and heart problems.

11.4 Birch leaves

Folium Betulae
Preparation: Healing tea (infusion)
This tea is diuretic and helps against kidney ailments, gout and cleans the blood, also helps with bacterial and inflammatory urinary tract diseases, kidney grief and rheumatic complaints.
Pour 2 tablespoons of crushed birch leaves into 250 ml of boiling water, let stand for 10 minutes. Then sieve.
Drink one cup of it a day.

11.5 Buckeye

Aesculus hippocastanum, fol.
Preparation: Different effects
Good for varicose veins, wrinkles, hemorrhoids, rheumatic complaints, menstrual problems, convulsions.
Active ingredients: Aesculus saponins, tannins, flvonglycosides
Nit use in pregnancy, sensitive stomach.

11.6 Burdock root

Radix Bardanae
Preparation: Healing tea (infusion)
For urinary tract infections, edema, lymphatic stasis, urinary troches, eczema, influenza infections, rheumatic arthritis, gout, varicose veins.
10g / Liter
One of the best blood cleaners. Many toxins are excreted from the liver via the gallbladder, but some are excreted via the blood. The burdock root has the unique ability to release toxins through the bloodstream and helps to detoxify the liver.
Medical applications: abscesses, acne, anger, arthritis, blood cleansing, boils, bronchitis, lip ulcers, cancer, candida, chickenpox, colds, cough, bladder catarrh, dandruff, edema, eczema, gynecology, fever, flu, gout, hay fever, hives, hypoglycemia , Indigestion, inhibits tumors, irritability, jaundice, swollen joints, keratosis, kidney and liver problems, lymph congestion, measles, mumps, goat peter, obesity, pain, pneumonia, psoriasis, rheumatism, scabies, skin diseases, throat infections, sprains, staphylococci, urinary tract infections, uterine prolapse.
Properties: Alterative (gradually restores health), antibacterial, antibiotic, antifungal, anti-inflammatory, antipyretic, antitumoral, laxative, stimulates sex drive, choleretic, soothing, sweat-inducing, lactating, hypoglycemic, muco-stimulating, nourishing, rejuvenating.

11.7 Chicory roots

Cichorium intybus, rad.
Preparation: Decoction
Helps against jaundice, hepatitis, fever, nausea, diarrhea, headache, constipation, dry stools, thirst, bloating, loss of appetite,
mood swings, edema, obesity, hyperuricemia (gout and rheumatism).
2-6 grams of finely chopped root are doused with 150 ml of cold water.
Cook for 2 - 3 minutes and then strain. The tea is drunk ½ hour before the meal and should not be sweetened.
In rare cases, allergic skin reactions may occur.

11.8 Chili pods

Capsicum annuum, fruct.
Preparation: Embrocation
Externally as rubs well against rheumatic diseases, colds, fever, indigestion, nausea, vomiting, pain, depression, tension.
High doses may lead to life-threatening hypothermia, prolonged use, acute gastritis, inflammation of the kidneys. Capsicum preparations irritate the skin and mucous membranes even in small quantities and may cause painful burning sensations.

11.9 Eucalyptus

Eucalyptus globulus
Preparation: Decoction
Good against airway inflammation with mucilage, flu, infections, muscle pain, headache, inflammation of the urinary tract, rheumatic complaints.
9-15 g
Use: tea, essential oil
Not for children under the age of 12 or in the first trimester of pregnancy.

11.10   Gentian root

Gentiana scabra
Preparation: Healing tea (infusion)
Has a decongestant, lowers the fever, strengthens the stomach, relieves pain and inflammation in rheumatism.
Drink 2-5 g in two doses after meals
Powder 2-3 g pur, take as capsules or infusion in two doses after meals
Specialties: Gentian has been used in both Eastern and Western medicine for a very long time as bitter tonic. It stimulates digestion and increases blood circulation in the abdomen. Gentian calms the overactive energies of the spleen and pancreas and may delay the development of diabetes. It also prevents pre-existing diabetes mellitus from progressing

11.11   Ginkgo leaves

Ginkgo biloba
Preparation: Decoction
Highly effective antioxidant. Good against cerebral circulatory disorders, high blood pressure, angina pectoris, atherosclerosis, asthma, shortness of breath.
Studies prove the effect of Ginkgo Bilboa concentrate as a highly effective antioxidant, which can protect healthy cells against side effects

of the chemotherapy drug adriamycin. Ginkgo has a tumor-inhibiting effect in cultures of oral and liver cancer cells and protected rats from chemically induced colon cancer in animal experiments.

11.12   Horsetail

Herba Equiseti
Preparation: Healing tea (infusion)
Significant blood-stilling effect. Put Compresses or nasal tampons with a decoction on the affected body zones.
40-50g of the plant per liter of water. Allow to boil for 10 minutes at slow heat. Drink 3-5 cups daily.
German Synonyms: horsetail, scouring rush, cattail Occurrence: Europe and America. Grows in cool, humid and bright locations of temperate climates. Sometimes it can also be found on rocky terrain, along roadsides and other dry places. Preferably loamy soil.
External application: Compression. They are prepared with a more concentrated decoction (100-150 g per liter of water) (see instructions above). Place the compresses on the affected body zones, e.g. On the chest or the anus. Nasal tampons. They are impregnated with the more concentrated decoction and introduced coldly into the nose.
Fresh juice. It is obtained by pressing out the plant. 3 tablespoons of each meal.

11.13   Juniper berries

Juniperus, fruct.
Preparation: Decoction
Promotes digestion. Good for loss of appetite, fatigue, rheumatism, gout, immune deficiency, irritable bladder.
Pour 2 teaspoons of the tea into 250 ml of boiling water and leave for 10 minutes. Then sieve. Drink 2 to 3 cups per day as needed.
Use: tea, season
Avoid overdose, pregnant women and acute kidney patients should do without. External rubbing may cause blistering of the skin.

11.14   Nettle leaves

Herba Urticae
Preparation: Healing tea (infusion)
Appetizing, Purifying, Hemostatic, Diarrhea, promotes blood formation, Promotes hair growth, Diuretic, Urinary tract disorders, Rheumatism, Expectorant, Metabolism, Rheumatism, Arthritis, Hypoglycemic, Detoxifying.

Add 2-4 teaspoons of the tea to 250 ml of boiling water and infuse for 10 minutes. Then sieve. Drink 2 to 3 cups per day as needed.
Active Ingredients: Flavonoids, Chlorophylls, Vitamins, Mineral Salts, Beta-Sistosterol, Plant Acid, Histamine in the Hair,

11.15   Nettle root

Urtica dioica, rad.
Preparation: Different effects
Stabilizes urinary behavior. Good for rheumatism and gout

11.16   Reishi

Ganoderma lucidum
Preparation: Different effects
Regenerates the liver, has a detoxifying and anti-inflammatory effect. Good for chronic hepatitis, swelling, redness and itching. Regulates the immune system, awakens and supports the self-healing powers.
Improves the oxygen saturation of the blood.
As an addition to tea, cocoa or coffee. As capsules, extract, powder or whole mushroom.

11.17   Rooibos

Aspalathus linearis
Preparation: Healing tea (infusion)
Antioxidant, anti-inflammatory, anti-cancer, protects against flavonoids, also has a positive effect on Alzheimer's, arteriosclerosis. Antiallergic, inhibits histamine release. Antibacterial, antiviral, antifungal, detoxifying (alkaline).
Brew 3-4 teaspoons of rooibos with one liter of boiling water and leave for 6-10 minutes. With soft water you need less tea for the preparation, with harder water we recommend a higher dosage.

11.18   Sorrel

Rumex crispus, rad. / Rumex acetosa herb.
Preparation: Different effects
Helps against skin diseases (eczema), itching, ulcers, swollen glands, constipation, liver and gland disease, rheumatic diseases, gout, iron deficiency.
Pour fresh or dried leaves with water and leave to soak for at least ten minutes.
Do not use during pregnancy and lactation.

11.19   St. Benedict's thistle, blessed thistle

Centaurea benedicta
Preparation: Healing tea (infusion)
The oil of the plant, which has been used in purulent skin ulcers, has a bacteriostatic action against staphylococci. Attention: The thistle has a certain allergy potential.
The Benedictine herb has a certain allergy potential. The oil of the plant, which was used in purulent skin ulcers, acts bacteriostatic especially against staphylococci.

11.20   Willow bark

salix alba
Preparation: Healing tea (infusion)
Antipyretic, anti-inflammatory, analgesic.
9-15 g

12 Basics of Nutrition

The basic principles of nutrition described herein are general recommendations. They are not aimed at a specific form of therapy. Recommendations concerning a therapy have priority.

12.1 Nutrition

Regular meals in a relaxed atmosphere. A warm breakfast is considered a good start into the day.

The main meals ought to be taken for lunch – supper in the early evening. Pay attention to feeling hungry or sated: don't eat too much nor remain hungry is the rule

Prepare the meals freshly from natural, regional products. Frozen, heat-conserved, industrially prepared or foodstuffs cooked in the microwave oven are rejected.

Choice of foodstuffs according to the season: more cooling food in summer, more warming food in winter.

Eat cooked food at least twice a day. Food and drinks ought to be lukewarm, never ice-cold or hot.

Raw vegetables, briefly cooked vegetables, freshly squeezed juices and mineral water are not recommended. Milk and dairy products are only included in the diet if they don't cause problems.

Don't use therapeutic recipes over a longer period without consulting your doctor or therapist.

Varied food

Enjoy the diversity of foodstuffs. Characteristics of a balanced nutrition are variety, suitable combination and a balanced quantity of rich and low energy foodstuffs (on one hand avoiding undersupply with essential nutrients and on the other hand to take to many undesirable substances)

A lot of Cereal Products - and Potatoes

Bread, pasta, rice, cereal flakes (best wholemeal) as well as potatoes contain almost no fat, but many vitamins, mineral nutrients, trace elements, roughage and secondary plant substances. These foodstuffs ought to be taken with low-fat side dishes.

Vegetables and Fruit – „Take Five" every day …

5 portions of vegetables and fruit a day, as fresh as possible, briefly cooked, or maybe one portion as a juice – ideal as a side dish to every meal as well as snack between meals: Thus a lot of vitamins, mineral nutrients as well as roughage and secondary plant substances

Daily milk and dairy products
Milk and Dairy Products every Day, once or twice per Week Fish; meat, sausages as well as eggs moderately. These foodstuffs contain valuable nutrients like calcium in the milk, iodine selenium and omega-3 fat acids in saltwater fish. Meat is favorable due to its high content of disposable iron and the vitamins B1, B6 and B12. Quantities of 300 – 600 g meat and sausage per week are sufficient. Prefer low-fat products, especially in meat- and dairy products.

Low-fat and fatty Foodstuffs
Fat supplies us with essential fat acids and fatty foodstuffs contain also fat-soluble vitamins. Fat is high in energy; therefore much fat in the food may cause overweight, possibly also cancer. Too many saturated fat acids may further a tendency for cardio-vascular diseases in the long term. Prefer vegetable oils and fats (e.g. rapeseed-, olive-, soya-oils and solid fats produced therefrom). Beware of invisible fat in meat- and dairy products, pastry and sweets as well as in fast-food and convenience foods. 70 – 90 g fat per day is sufficient.

Moderately Sugar and Salt
Take sugar and foods/drinks containing various kinds of sugar (e.g. glucose syrup) only occasionally. Use herbs and spices as well as a little salt creatively. Prefer salt containing iodine.

Plenty of Liquids
Water is absolutely essential. Drink 1-2 l liquids every day. Prefer water (with or without gas) and other low-calorie drinks. Alcoholic drinks should not be taken.

Tasty Dishes, carefully cooked
Cook the meals with as low temperatures and as short as possible, using little water and fat – this preserves the original taste, keeps the nutrients intact and prevents the production of harmful compounds.

Take time and enjoy the food
Take your Time and enjoy your Food
Eating consciously helps to eat right. The eye enjoys food, too. It's fun, invites to enjoy varied dishes and stimulates the feeling of satiety.

Watch your Weight and stay in Motion
A balanced diet and a lot of exercise and sport (30 – 60 min/day) are a healthy combination. The right weight furthers well-being and health. Thermals, directional effectiveness, digestive power

There are various criteria for judging the effectiveness of herbs and foodstuffs.

The use of certain herbs and ingredients is based on observations of the effects on the body which these foodstuffs, herbs and spices show after having eaten them. The medical science has developed following system: Every ingredient or herb has a directional effectiveness. Furthermore, there are herbs which have a special effect on certain organs.

The basic condition for a healthy metabolism is to obtain sufficient energy from food and that the digestive process doesn't use too much energy.

An easily digestible meal makes content and sated, doesn't cause flatulence and fatigue after the meal. The perfect spices increase the healthiness of our meals. Very often, just small doses of herbs and spices will suffice. They are not used to make us sated, but to help our digestive organs to digest the food.

12.2 Recipes

The recipes list the ingredients to be used and the cooking instructions show how the dish is prepared. The list of ingredients shows the concerned quantities as well as the relevance for the therapy. If you find „less than mentioned", try to comply or find an alternative from the „list of recommended foodstuffs". Mostly it shall result just in a small change of taste when you simply avoid this ingredient.

Mild cooking methods: boiling, stewing, poaching, steaming
Strong cooking methods: barbecuing, roasting, frying, smoking
Balanced cooking methods: deep-frying, baking brick
Deep-freezing and warming in the microwave oven should be avoided (denaturalization).

12.3 Foodstuffs

Foodstuffs have an effect on body and soul like medicinal herbs, only a very much milder one. Dietary advice is mainly based on regional foodstuffs. The knowledge about the effects of each foodstuff and the knowledge, when which foodstuff shall be used, is based on the orthodox school of medicine. Use ecologic-organic products, if possible. As everything should be cooked for a long time due to a better digestability and very rarely eaten raw, the food agrees with everyone.

The classification of the foodstuffs according to their effect on the body is the basis in order to achieve a harmonious status of health.

Dietary advisors do not recommend certain foodstuffs for everyone. The individual diet is tailor-made for the individual constitution.

Buy only fresh and ripe fruit and vegetables. You ought to leave unripe fruit and vegetables and such with brown spots and wilted leaves behind in the market. In this case take deep-frozen goods (never ready-to-serve dishes!). Fruit and vegetables are deep-frozen immediately after harvesting and often contain more vitamins and minerals than the goods from the vegetable shelf. Whereas conserved or tinned goods contain very much less biological substances. Also, salt, sugar and others are mostly added to the latter. Never leave the foodstuffs in the water after washing them to avoid that many vital substances get drowned. Clean salads, fruit and vegetables immediately before serving.

Please make sure of the hygienic processing of foodstuffs. Clean your salads, fruit and vegetables carefully. When cooking with meat, prepare all ingredients first and then process the meat products. Clean the worktop and tools very carefully. Wooden surfaces ought to be treated with a mild disinfectant regularly in order to reduce germination.

Store fruit and vegetables separately, if possible. Harvested fruit and vegetables are still alive and emit e.g. ethylene gas, which makes other products ripen and age faster. Keep meat and fish in the closed packaging or store them in the fridge in closed containers.

12.4 Herbs

There are some basic rules for storing medicinal herbs. On principle, herbs must be protected from direct sunlight, humidity and heat.

Containers for the storage of herbs may be glasses, ceramic jars and even plastic containers. However, plastic is a rather unsuitable material and should only be a short-term solution. In case of glass containers, use a dark material.

Medicinal herbs cannot be kept for any long period. The shelf life of herbs is limited. However, it can be prolonged with suitable storage. The place should be dark, rather cool and absolutely dry. A wooden medicine cabinet, placed not directly next to a source of heat, would be ideal. Never buy large quantities of herbs so as not to have to throw them away. Label the container with the name of the herb and the date of harvesting or processing.

13 Other dietic-books

The following syndromes of dietetics, TCM or for a therapy supplement for cancer are available.

Dietetics

E001. Nutrition of the infant - baby food
E002. Nutrition during lactation
E003. Nutrition in old age
E004. Nutrition of children and adolescents
E005. Nutrition of athletes
E006. Light weight
E007. Pregnancy
E008. Full food

Protein and electrolyte - kidneys
E009. (hemodialysis) dialysis treatment
E010. Acute renal failure
E011. Chronic renal insufficiency
E012. Nephrotic syndrome
E013. Kidney stones (nephrolithiasis)

Gastrointestinal tract - pancreas
E014. Acute pancreatitis (inflammation of the pancreas)
E015. Chronic pancreatitis (inflammation of the pancreas)

Gastrointestinal tract - small intestine and large intestine
E016. Acute obstipation (constipation)
E017. Chronic obstipation (constipation)
E018. Colon irritabile
E019. Diverticulitis
E020. Acquired lactose intolerance (lactose malabsorption)
E021. Fructose malabsorption
E022. Glutensensitive enteropathy (celiac disease)
E023. Colectomy
E024. Short Bowel Syndrome

Gastrointestinal tract - liver, gallbladder, bile ducts
E025. Acute and chronic hepatitis (inflammation of the liver)
E026. Cholelithiasis (bile stones)
E027. fatty liver
E028. cirrhosis

Gastrointestinal tract - Stomach and duodenal intestine
E029. Acute gastritis
E030. Chronic gastritis
E031. Stomach bleeding
E032. Ulcus ventriculi and duodenal ulcer
E033. Condition after gastric surgery

Gastrointestinal tract - oral cavity and esophagus
E034. Stomatitis
E035. Esophageal carcinoma (esophageal cancer)
E036. Refluosophagitis (heartburn)

Special diseases
E037. Phenylketonuria (PKU)
E038. Rheumatic joint diseases

Metabolism
E039. Obesity (overweight)
E040. Diabetes mellitus
E041. Eating disorders (underweight)

Fat metabolism
E042. Hypercholesterolaemia (increased cholesterol level)
E043. Hepatic Encephalopathy

Heart and circulation
E044. Arteriosclerosis (arterial calcification)
E045. Heart insufficiency
E046. Hypertension
E047. Hyperuricaemia and gout

Changed nutrient requirements
E048. In case of fever
E049. For malignant diseases
E050. After burns
E051. Radiation and chemotherapy

CANCER
E100. Pancreatic cancer
E101. Bladder cancer
E102. Blood cancer (leukemia)
E103. Breast cancer
E104. Colorectal cancer
E105. Gastric cancer
E106. Kidney cancer
E107. Esophageal cancer

TCM
E200. Bladder - moisture heat in the bladder
E201. Bladder - moisture and cold in the bladder
E202. Bladder - emptiness and cold in the bladder
E203. Large intestine - external cold affects the large intestine
E204. Large intestine - moisture heat in the large intestine
E205. Large intestine - heat blocks the intestine II acute
E206. Large intestine - dryness of the colon
E207. Large intestine - Yang deficiency (cold)
E208. Heart - Blood insufficiency
E209. Heart - Blood stagnation
E210. Heart - Fire
E211. Heart - Hot mucus clogs the heart pores

E212. Heart - Cold mucus clogs the heart pores
E213. Heart - Qi deficiency
E214. Heart - Yang deficiency
E215. Heart - Yin deficiency
E216. Liver - Ascending Liver Yang
E217. Liver - Blood deficiency
E218. Liver - Blood stagnation
E219. Liver - Moisture heat in liver and gall bladder
E220. Liver - Fire
E221. Liver - Gall bladder Qi-Empty
E222. Liver - Cold in the liver meridian
E223. Liver - Qi stagnation
E224. Liver - Wind
E225. Liver - Wind with ascending liver Yang
E226. Liver - Wind with blood anemic
E227. Liver - Wind with extreme heat
E228. Lung - Qi deficiency
E229. Lung - Mucus-moisture in the lungs
E230. Lung - Mucus-heat in the lungs
E231. Lung - Mucus-cold in the lungs
E232. Lung - Dryness of the lungs
E233. Lung - Wind-heat attacks the lungs
E234. Lung - Wind-cold affects the lungs
E235. Lung - Yin deficiency
E236. Stomach - Bloodstagnation
E237. Stomach - Fire
E238. Stomach - Cold with liquid
E239. Stomach - Nutrition stagnation
E240. Stomach - Qi deficiency
E241. Stomach - Rebellious Qi
E242. Stomach - Yin Emptiness
E243. Spleen - Heat and moisture attack the spleen
E244. Spleen - Coldness and moisture affects the spleen
E245. Spleen - Qi deficiency
E246. Spleen - Qi deficiency + Declining spleen Qi
E247. Spleen - Qi deficiency + spleen does not control the blood
E248. Spleen - Yang deficiency
E249. Kidney - Heart and kidney no longer communicate
E250. Kidney - Jing deficiency
E251. Kidney - Kidneys cannot receive the Qi
E252. Kidney - Qi is not stable
E253. Kidney - Yang deficiency
E254. Kidney - Yin deficiency

For further information visit di-book.com.

14 EBNS - Software for nutritional counseling

The main task of the database is to create personalized nutritional advice
for each patient individually. The database was developed for Dietetics

and Traditional Chinese Medicine.
The Database supports training and advices in the daily work routine.

The computer program provides lists of recipes, ingredients and herbs, which are given to the client. individually adjustable according to patient's request from whole food to vegetarians (lacto, ovo, ...). For every register there is an information sheet which can be given to the client. All texts can be individually designed.

The syndromes can be combined and result in an intersection of the recommended recipes and ingredients. The automated diagnosis for the TCM enables you to check your experience during the training as well as to confirm your diagnosis in the working day. You select several predefined symptoms and have the program automatically display the relevant syndromes.

How to work with the database:
Select the patient / client, select one or more of the syndromes you diagnosed and print the folder.

You can change all values, create new symptoms or syndromes, develop recipes, change or adapt ingredients and herbs to your findings. In simple client management, all relevant data about the person is stored. You get an overview of the past diagnoses and the development of the course of the disease.

As a consultant you save a lot of time when you print out the recipe, food and herbal lists for the recognized syndromes and give them to the clients. You can use this time for a personal conversation. With the database, dieticians and nutritionists can view the nutrients and trace elements for each recipe and develop recipes for syndromes even with suggested ingredients.

All recipe and grocery lists can also be ordered from me as a combination of several diseases. I wish all readers good luck, health and happiness in life.
More information can be found at www.ebns.at.
Volunteer: www.krebsinfo.at
Josef Miligui